Hallucinogenic and Poisonous Mushroom
FIELD GUIDE

by Gary P. Menser

AND/OR PRESS
Berkeley, California
1977

This *Guide* is not a substitute for experience and professional training. DO NOT CONSUME ANY MUSHROOMS UNLESS THEIR IDENTITY HAS BEEN CONFIRMED BY A MYCOLOGIST. The Author and Publisher of this book advise against and take no responsibility for anyone consuming wild mushrooms.

Color Photography:

Kit Scates: Galerina autumnalis, Amanita phalloides, Amanita pantherina, Gymnopilus spectabilis, Panaeolina foenisecii, Panaeolus campanulatus, Panaeolus fimicola, Panaeolus semiovatus, Panaeolus phalaenarum, Panaeolus subbalteatus, Psilocybe pelliculosa.

Bob Harris: Amanita muscaria, Panaeolus acuminatus, Panaeolus retirugis, Panaeolus subbalteatus, Psilocybe baeocystis, Psilocybe stuntzii.

J.Q. Jacobs: Psilocybe baeocystis, Psilocybe coprophila, Psilocybe cyanescens, Psilocybe cyanescens, Psilocybe pelliculosa, Psilocybe semilanceata, Psilocybe stuntzii.

Jeremy Bigwood: Psilocybe cubensis.

All others by author.

Acknowledgements

The author sincerely appreciates and acknowledges the technical assistance of Bill Sweet, Kit Scates, Paul Vergeer and Bill Burley; their advice has helped formulate my ideas and made this book possible. I wish to thank the illustrators whose collaboration was necessary. Finally special thanks goes to Terry and Scylla for their time and typing skills, and Tia, whose assistance and patience was, once again, indispensable.

Published and distributed by
And/Or Press
Box 2246
Berkeley, Ca., 94702

Book Design by Hal Hershey
Cover Photo Gary Menser
Line Drawings by Michael B. Smith
Typesetting by Richard Ellington

1st Printing June 1977
2nd Printing June 1978
3rd Printing October 1979
4th Printing October 1980

Contents

Introduction

The mushrooms of the West share features with mushrooms found throughout the world. Some are edible, some are poisonous and some are psychoactive. The author of this book neither advocates nor condemns their consumption. Documented accounts show that they have been used for thousands of years for cooking, religious purposes and intoxication.

Any substance capable of producing alteration of consciousness arouses controversy, and controversy gives rise to myth. Science has an obligation to replace myth with fact. Hopefully this book will serve as a step towards that goal. *Poison,* for example, has a very specific definition in the glossary. *Psychoactive* has an entirely separate definition.

The term *hallucinogenic,* when applied to the altered state of consciousness achieved through ingestion of mushrooms, is very misleading. Hallucinations have long been associated with schizophrenic and psychotic behavior. Inherent in this behavior is a disassociation from reality. The psychotic or schizophrenic truly believes that his hallucinatory world exists. Hallucinations brought on by the ingestion of psychoactive mushrooms should be more accurately termed pseudo-hallucinogenic. The pseudo-hallucination is perceived but evaluated as fictitious. *Psychotomimetic* ('mimic of psychosis') is the word most often found in the scientific literature. But the altered state does not quite mimic the naturally occurring schizophrenias, and those who ingest mushrooms do not become psychotic. The term *psychedelic* ('mind manifesting') seems to interpret the state without being judgmental about the effects. However, I chose to use the term *psychoactive* ('capable of altering nervous system functioning') throughout this book, since it describes the qualities of the mushrooms and not the experiences they produce.

This book is intended as a field guide for the identification of the various genera and species of psychoactive and deadly poisonous mushrooms found primarily in the western half of North America, excluding Mexico. The locations given represent only the known distribution. This constantly changes as we learn of new locations. The amateur should read the entire book (including the macroscopic glossary) before attempting to gather and identify mushrooms, since many species share very similar characteristics. For example, the deadly *Galerinas* have rusty brown spore prints as does *Conocybe cyanopus*. Confusing these two mushrooms could have lethal results if samples were ingested in quantity. Short of expert microscopic evaluation, some mushrooms can only be identified through chemical analysis.

Anyone can obtain qualitative chemical analysis of dried mushrooms. The analysis will confirm or deny the presence of psilocybin and/or psilocin. Tests will also indicate whether or not the mushrooms have been adulterated with LSD, as black market mushrooms sometimes are. To obtain quantitative analysis (percent or amount present) you must first be registered with the Drug Enforcement Administration. Analysis can be done for a fee* by PharmChem Laboratories, a non-profit organization.

I want to stress again that anyone collecting mushrooms should follow strict identification procedures. Ingestion of only one mushroom in some species of *Amanita* can be lethal. All of the mushrooms in the book which are referred to as poisonous are potentially lethal.

*For Oregon residents, this fee is paid by the Drug Information Center at the University of Oregon. The addresses of these two organizations are listed on page 96.

What Are Mushrooms?

Toadstools and mushrooms are one and the same. They are considered to be the *fruiting bodies* of the mushroom plant. These fruiting bodies produce the spores that reproduce the species. Spores are produced on the gills *(hymenium)* of the mushroom and when ripe they are discharged, to blow in the wind.

The actual plant is usually under the ground, in dung or wood. It is called the *vegetative portion* and is composed of microscopic filaments called *hyphae*. When these filaments are found in a mass, they are called *mycelium*. The fruiting body grows out of and derives its nourishment from the mycelium.

The mycelium gets its food from organic matter by producing enzymes that break down complex compounds. These by-products are then absorbed, and used by the hyphae as food to promote growth. The mycelium will continue to grow as long as a proper combination of environmental conditions and nutrients exists. Little is known about these conditions except that a great deal of water is necessary. Mushrooms are composed of about 90% water, and the majority will fruit after it rains. Often heavy fog will condense and provide enough moisture for fruiting.

Mycelium occurs in many different habitats. When the growth takes place in wood it is called *lignicolous*. This may take place in trees, stumps, branches or buried wood. Mushrooms growing out of the ground but not on wood or dung are called *terrestrial*. The third type of growth takes place in dung and is called *coprophilous*. Many times dung is washed into the soil or grass and

Mushroom Parts

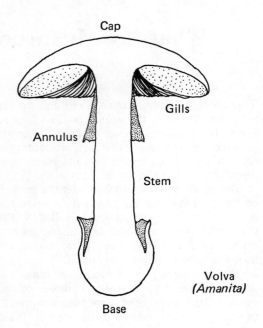

Cap

Gills

Annulus

Stem

Volva
(Amanita)

Base

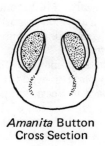

Amanita Button
Cross Section

only a close observation will show the true habitat. Certain dung-inhabiting species are made more viable when the spores have passed through an animal before germination.

Most mycelium looks the same, so identification of fungi is based on the characteristics of the fruiting body and its spores, not the vegetative portion.

Mushrooms, or the vegetative mycelium are not plants in the literal sense. They lack chlorophyll and therefore cannot convert the sun's energy into food like ᵗrue plants do. Sustenance depends upon organic matter, either dead or alive.

The fungi living on dead organic matter are called *saprophytes*. Their ecological function is to break down organic matter. If the forests had no fungi, the earth would be crowded with dead trees. There is as much energy in dead organic matter as it took to grow it.

Sometimes fungi will invade a living plant or tree and will weaken or kill it by taking away its nourishment. This type of fungi is called a parasite.

A third fungal relationship is called the *mycorrhizal association*. This is a symbiotic relationship between fungus and plant or tree roots. The fungus increases the plant's nutritional intake in return for sustenance. In this instance, as with some lignicolous mushrooms, spores play a minor role, as the mushrooms will return, usually every year. For this reason many of our mushrooms are associated with certain types of trees. In some cases, there may be a relationship with grass roots.

The mushrooms described in this book belong to one of the three groups described above.

How to Collect, Identify and Dry

For best results the only equipment necessary for the hunt is a knife, some wax paper and a basket. The knife is used to dig up the mushrooms. Many times the base has important distinguishing characteristics. Care should be taken to get the whole plant; don't break it off. Dig it up—it may indicate the habit and what it is growing from. Wax paper is used to wrap the species, and keep them separated; it also allows them to breathe. Mushrooms will keep best when placed in a basket, providing they don't smash each other. The sweating produced by the use of plastic bags can ruin a day's collection. The idea is to keep the mushrooms from becoming too wet or smashed.

If hunting on private land, permission should be secured beforehand, otherwise you may be trespassing.

Before collecting notice the manner of growth. This is called the habit. When mushrooms are all by themselves, they are called *solitary*. When they are grouped one or two feet apart they are considered to be *scattered*. *Gregarious* mushrooms grow in groups, not in a clustered manner but close together. If growth occurs aggregated in tufts, but not growing together, it is called *cespitose*.

Next notice the natural place of growth. This is called the *habitat*. Habitats of the mushroom species in this book are either dung (coprophilous), wood (lignicolous) or the ground (terrestrial). These habitats mainly occur in mixed woods, conifer forests, pasture lands, lawns and woodchips.

Cap

Dig up the mushroom, being careful to get the whole fruiting body, then examine the cap. Try to get maximum and minimum measurements and notice the variations. Study the different shapes of the cap and the difference between young and old mushrooms. Notice the effect that age has on the color. The moisture content with many mushrooms affects the color as well. When this happens it is called *hygrophanous.*

Look for stains that may develop during handling. The surface of the cap may be smooth or *striate* (with radiating lines or furrows) and there may or may not be a *pellicle* attached. The pellicle is a skinlike layer on the surface of the cap of most of the *Psilocybe* species that can, in a moist condition, be separated.

Some caps are viscid to the touch in moist weather. The margin or outer edge of the cap may be incurved or straight. This should be observed in both young and old specimens. It may be raised or wavy. The margin may or may not have the remains of a protective covering that covered the gills at an early age. This is called the *partial veil.*

Notice the consistency of the cap. Is it soft or firm, brittle or pliant?

Stem

Measure the length and width of the stem and notice the range of variations compared with other similar species. The shape may be equal or subequal, bulbous, straight or sinuous. The color may change as it ages. The surface may be smooth, striate or covered with a white powder. Sometimes the remnants of the partial veil that once covered the gills will remain on the stem as an *annulus* or fibrils, and is often darkened by falling spores.

The top of the stem may be flared or striate. The base may be enlarged or bent and have roots attached or it may be covered with white mycelium. Watch to see if the mycelium changes to blue. If the base is enlarged and has a volva then you probably have an *Amanita*.

Check the consistency. Is the stem pliant, or will it break with a snap? Cut a stem in half and check to see whether it is solid or hollow and whether it contains a brown pith.

Gills

Notice the color of the gills and the difference between young and old mushrooms. See if the gills are mottled. Examine the top of the stem and observe the attachment between the stem and gills. Attachment can be *adnate* (broadly attached), *adnexed* (narrowly attached), *uncinate* (hooked), *free* (not attached to the stem), or *decurrent* (running down).

Look at the edge of the gill. The edge may be pale or white and might have a cottony substance. This is the product of sterile cells called *cheilocystidia*. When the fruiting bodies become mature the spores often darken the edge and it may be harder to view.

The spacing of the gills is very important. Gill spacing is divided into three groups and two intergrades. When the gills are very close it is called *crowded*. Between crowded and *distant* is *close*. The intergrades are called *subclose* and *subdistant*.

This checklist is intended for use in the field. The notes taken when the collection is made will be a necessary tool for identification after a spore color is determined. If you wait until you have made a spore print your fresh specimens won't be fresh any more and identification becomes much more difficult. It is strongly recommended that notes be taken in the field and keyed on the spot to the mushroom gathered.

All measurements are in metrics. Refer to the ruler printed on the back of this book for taking field measurements. The metric system is very easy to understand; just remember that ten millimeters equals one centimeter and two centimeters is close to an inch.

1. **BEFORE COLLECTING** any mushroom notice these things.

   A. Habit
   1. Solitary
   2. Scattered
   3. Gregarious
   4. Cespitose

   B. Habitat
   1. Coprophilous (on dung)
   2. Lignicolous (on wood)
   3. Terrestrial (on the ground)
   4. Mixed woods
   5. Conifer forests
   6. Pasture lands or grass

2. **COLLECTING** the mushroom.

   Dig it up, don't pick it. The advantages are:
   1. Sometimes the base is needed to determine the species.
   2. It may help in determining the habit.
   3. It may help in determining the habitat.

3. Examining the **CAP**.

   A. Size
   1. Maximum
   2. Minimum
   3. Variations

   B. Shape
   1. Young
   2. Old
   3. Variations

   C. Color
   1. Young
   2. Old
   3. Variations
   4. Wet and dry states
   5. Stains in bruising or drying.

   D. Surface
   1. Smooth
   2. Striate
   3. Pellicle present
   4. Viscid

   E. Margin
   1. Incurved
   2. Straight
   3. Raised
   4. Wavy
   5. Striate
   6. Veil remnants

   F. Consistency
   1. Soft
   2. Pliant
   3. Firm
   4. Thin
   5. Thick

4. Examining the **STEM**.

    A. Size
       1. Length, range
       2. Width, range

    B. Shape
       1. Equal or subequal
       2. Straight
       3. Flattened
       4. Sinuous
       5. Bulbous

    C. Color
       1. Young
       2. Old
       3. Stains

    D. Surface
       1. Smooth
       2. Striate
       3. Covered with a white powder
       4. Annulus or veil remnants

    E. Apex
       1. Flared
       2. Striate

    F. Base
       1. Enlarged
       2. Bent
       3. Roots
       4. Covered with white mycelium
       5. Staining (color)
       6. Volva *(Amanita)*

    G. Consistency
       1. Pliant
       2. Cartilaginous
       3. Fragile
       4. Solid
       5. Hollow
       6. Stuffed with pith

5. Examining the **GILLS**.

    A. Color
       1. Young
       2. Old
       3. Mottled

    B. Attachment
       1. Adnate
       2. Adnexed
       3. Uncinate
       4. Free
       5. Decurrent

C. Edge
  1. White or paler
  2. With a cottony substance
  3. Same color as gills

D. Spacing
  1. Crowded
  2. Subclose
  3. Close
  4. Subdistant
  5. Distant

Now that you have made notes on your observations of the mushroom parts, you can narrow your search down to genus by making a spore print. The color of the spores in mass will sometimes indicate what genus you have.

How to Make a Spore Print

Remove the stem and place the mushroom gills down on paper. Any white paper is adequate, but sometimes a "white" deposit, e.g. *Amanita* spores, can be seen better on black paper. For best results place a glass or equivalent over the mushroom. Covering the cap prevents drying out of specimens. Placing a drop or two of water on the cap will also help retard the drying process. This is more important with the smaller species. Wait several hours or overnight, then check the color on the paper under the mushroom. The color of a spore print will change in time so the color of the fresh print is most important.

Note that spore prints of some psychoactive and poisonous genera and species are the same, which makes supporting identification even more imperative.

Spore colors of the psychoactive genera:

Amanita	White
Conocybe	Rusty brown to ochraceous
Gymnopilus	Rusty orange
Panaeolina	Dark purple brown
Panaeolus	Black
Psilocybe	Purplish, dark lavender gray or purple brown

Spore colors of the poisonous species of the West.

Amanita bisporigera	White
Amanita ocreata	White
Amanita phalloides	White
Amanita verna	White
Conocybe filaris	Rusty brown
Galerina autumnalis	Rusty brown
Galerina marginata	Rusty brown
Galerina venenata	Rusty brown

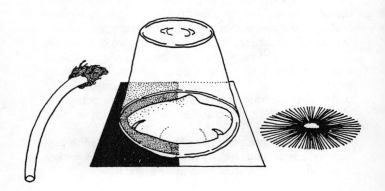

How to Make a Spore Print

Drying

Quite often, in cases described as mushroom poisoning, the culprit is not the mushrooms but bacteria that have grown because of improper drying methods.

In drying mushrooms, heat is not as important as most people think. The important thing is air circulation. This allows for a constant evaporation of moisture. Too much heat can cause the outer surface to seal moisture inside, thus retarding the drying process.

Mushrooms should not be washed with water prior to drying. This will just add to the water content. They should be cleaned by hand of all debris and dirt. If they are cut into smaller pieces moisture can evaporate from more surfaces and drying time will be less. Humidity is also a factor to consider. If you try to dry mushrooms in a place where humidity is high, drying time will be longer. Drying time decreases when less moisture is in the air.

The best method for preserving the psychoactive potency is freeze drying. An oven is a bad place to dry mushrooms. If the heat is above 100° F. the process of extracting moisture content is retarded severely.

Making a dryer is a very simple task. The idea is to provide an environment where air (not necessarily heat) can circulate. Fans are efficient for moving air, but they create more circulation than is really required, unless the fan is very small. Light bulbs provide an efficient means for extracting moisture. Heat rises, so if the light bulb is in a box, or whatever, under the mushrooms, air will circulate upwards. Hot plates will accomplish the same goal but cost more to operate.

Crispness is the goal of the drying process; if the mushrooms bend instead of breaking, they are not dry enough. Stringing them together is efficient, as long as they are hung in a place where humidity is low and air can circulate freely. If drying on a screen, don't stack them on top of each other, since this retards evaporation.

Dried mushrooms are the only kind the laboratory will accept for chemical analysis. Drying may slightly decrease the psychoactive potency. Too much heat, light, or moisture also decrease potency, as does age. Once dried, store them in a jar with a tight lid, add a bay leaf or a few peppercorns to absorb any residual moisture, and keep in the freezer. All moisture must be removed or else bacterial growth can occur. Storing fresh mushrooms in honey or in a freezer is not a good idea.

Chemical Qualities

POISONOUS

Most fatal mushroom poisonings are due to the group of amatoxins and phallotoxins found in certain species of *Amanita, Galerina,* and one known *Conocybe* species. The mortality rate for people who have ingested the poisonous species is about 50% at present. Little progress in obtaining a completely effective antidote or therapy has been made, and experimental studies are meeting with little success. Once symptoms occur treatment is mostly supportive, with an unknown potential for recovery due to individual idiosyncratic reactions and the dosage ingested. Prevention of this form of poisoning is thought possible with extensive education, as most of these poisonous species are easily identified.

Symptoms occur between six and twenty-four hours after ingestion. Nausea, severe colic distress and watery diarrhea are first noticed. Violent vomiting and convulsions have also been observed. After these initial manifestations of toxic reactions, the symptoms subside and the individual's condition may appear to improve. In the next few days toxic effects will re-emerge, and are manifested by renal failure, coma, and vascular collapse. In some cases, death has resulted within a week. Accurate information on dosage levels that can be ingested before toxic reactions occur is not available.

Chemical research has revealed two families of heat resistant cyclic peptides to be the basic constituents of the *Amanita* toxins: the amatoxins and phallotoxins. Of the two, the amatoxins are much more toxic than the

15

phallotoxins, and the effects of the latter are relatively insignificant when compared to the potency of the former (laboratory tests showed amatoxins to be lethal at extremely small concentrations—2 millionths of a gram of pure gamma-amanitin caused death in mice). Both types of poisons disrupt liver metabolism, and even if an individual recovers the possibility of permanent liver and kidney damage still exists.

Poisonous

Sac-like Volva

Typical Poisonous *Amanita* Mushroom
(one-half natural size)

Poisonous

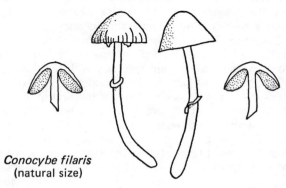

Conocybe filaris
(natural size)

Typical *Galerina* Mushroom
(natural size)

Poisonous species of *Amanita* contain amatoxins, with the majority also containing phallotoxins. The *Galerina* species contain amatoxins, as does one species of *Conocybe*. The quantity of a particular *Amanita* that would have to be ingested to produce death is not known with certainty, and will vary with the different species, but deaths have been reported as a result of the ingestion of as little as one *Amanita* mushroom. Not all the mushrooms with a saclike volva are poisonous, but all of the known poisonous ones do have this characteristic. It is thought that a lethal dosage of *Galerina* or *Conocybe* would be ten to twenty mushrooms. As is the case with most toxins, people of lesser weight will probably have more pronounced toxic reactions than those who are heavier. Pre-existing physical conditions may also be a factor in the overall prognosis.

PSYCHOACTIVE

Ibotenic Acid

Ibotenic acid and muscimol are the main chemical constituents of *Amanita muscaria* and *A. pantherina*. Ibotenic acid is one-tenth as strong as muscimol and, when ingested, the body rapidly changes some of the ibotenic acid to muscimol.

Ibotenic acid and muscimol have both been reported to resemble LSD in their influence on the levels of neural transmitters in the rat brain. Both compounds alter brain serotonin levels. It is thought that this activity may be responsible for the increased sensory perceptions that have been reported from ingestion of ibotenic acid. Electroencephalographic alterations show reaction in the brain to be distinct from hallucinogens such as LSD, with the action being more like the anticholinergic drug atropine. Muscimol is not a true hallucinogen; it is a delirifacient ('capable of causing delirium'). Available pharmacological data on the effects of ibotenic acid and muscimol should deter recreational use.

Ingestion will produce physiological effects in 15 to 60 minutes lasting several hours. The initial symptoms reported are drowsiness, disorientation, and alteration of sensory perceptions. Pseudo-hallucinations may follow and possibly strong muscle spasms. If taken in large quantities the duration of the effects may be prolonged for 24 hours. The person who has ingested ibotenic acid usually has a normal recovery, with no reports of hangovers.

Ingestion of *Amanita muscaria* and *A. pantherina* may produce effects on the body that will not soon be forgotten. A number of the *Amanitas,* especially *A. pantherina,* could be deadly if vomiting, along with marked anticholinergic effects of acetylcholine, are not controlled. Anticholinergics counter the effects of acetylcholine. Acetylcholine and serotonin are cerebral neural transmitters. *A. muscaria,* which enjoys a misplaced reputation as an hallucinogen, is less toxic than *Amanita pantherina.*

In regard to the potential psychoactivity of ibotenic acid and muscimol found in *A. muscaria* and *A. pantherina,* it should be noted that time of year, environmental conditions, and other growth factors may alter the quantity of these agents in different specimens. In addition, critical individual body chemistry and tolerance levels should be known by an individual prior to ingesting *Amanitas.* Specialists consider the use of any *Amanita* for recreation to be hazardous, with many individuals reporting unpleasant side effects.

As with the psilocybin and/or psilocin-containing mushrooms, the potential consumer of edible mushrooms should be cautioned that ingestion of a hallucinogen can cause shifts in one's perceptions of "set" and "setting." ("set" refers to one's expectations of what will happen in situations; "setting" refers to perceptions of the social and physical environment.) When this effect is not anticipated, for example when psychoactive substances are ingested unintentionally, the effect can be initially disturbing with attendant psychic distress.

Serotonin

Most, if not all, species of *Panaeolus* and one species of *Panaeolina* contain serotonin. Serotonin is a neuro-transmitter found in various areas of the body. It is thought to regulate sensory perception, body temperature, and sleep. There are more than ten psychoactive chemicals structurally related to serotonin. Some of the more common ones are DMT, psilocybin and psilocin. It is thought that these products exert their psycho-activity by altering the serotonin levels in the brain, producing pseudo-hallucinogenic and other effects in the user. This is only one of many theories explaining the action of psychoactive substances on humans.

Mushrooms that contain serotonin are not thought to produce psychoactive effects when ingested, as the sero-tonin is believed to be destroyed in the gastrointestinal tract. Even if serotonin were introduced into the body by another route or administration (smoking mushrooms, for example) it is thought the serotonin would be unable to penetrate the "blood-brain" barrier, and thus would be rendered incapable of psychoactivity.

Psilocybin and Psilocin

Psilocybin and psilocin are both indole alkaloids which are closely related chemically. These alkaloids have been found in certain species of the genera *Psilocybe, Panaeolus, Panaeolina* and *Conocybe*. Ingestion of mushrooms containing psilocybin will cause the body to metabolize the alkaloid to psilocin, and when distributed to the brain, psilocin will produce effects less pronounced and of a shorter duration than those observed with LSD. Psilocin is more than twice as strong as psilocybin. Baeocystin and norbaeocystin are also suspected of being active substances; however, tests of pure samples of these compounds on human subjects are not yet reported in the literature. These two alkaloids are found only in certain species of the genus *Psilocybe*.

Research indicates that psilocin induces an altered state of perceptual awareness by interfering with the transmission of stimuli that regulate the processing of information. Studies to date show that while the alkaloids are effective in small concentrations (milligram amounts), no physical dependence results from the use of psilocin. Repeated consumption of these mushrooms can quickly produce increased tolerance, requiring higher dosages for psychoactivity. Smoking psilocybin or psilocin is not believed to cause psychoactivity other than psychological psychoactivity.

Physical effects induced by ingestion are: slight increases in body temperature, pulse, and blood pressure. Since the body temperature of young children can fluctuate extremely, care should be taken to prevent accidental ingestion.

There is no toxic reaction (or at most, an extremely minimal one) to the ingestion of psilocybin or psilocin. The greatest potential danger would be the inability to cope with a temporary loss of psychological equilibrium. The ingestion of these mushrooms has the capacity to affect mental "set" and "setting" (once again, "set" refers to one's expectations of what will happen in situations, and "setting" refers to perceptions of the social and physical environment). When these effects are not anticipated, for example when psychoactive substances are ingested unintentionally, the effect can be initially disturbing with attendant psychic distress.

In recent years, more and more people have been searching habitats for psychoactive mushrooms. The greatest danger of this practice appears to be the relative ignorance of these hunters in accurate identification of psilocybin and psilocin containing mushrooms prior to ingestion. Ingestion of these mushrooms for recreational use requires the user to assess three distinct areas: A) proper identification of the mushrooms to determine psilocybin and/or psilocin content and dosage; B) a thorough understanding of the effects in the body and knowledge of potential side effects; C) an awareness that

the environment and activities encountered after ingestion should be as free of anxiety as possible. In addition
to these three constraints, strict legal penalties apply for
private use, cultivation or distribution of these mushrooms. Analysis of *Psilocybe baeocystis* has sometimes
shown this species to be void of psilocybin and/or psilocin. The active substance or substances are unknown
and therefore not illegal. The *Amanitas* are completely
legal.

Other Mushrooms

Other mushrooms exist that have caused death, but
they are relatively few in number, and are not likely to
be confused with the psychoactive species. The spore
print is the safest method for the amateur to use in iden-
tifying mushrooms by genus. If large amounts of mushrooms are collected and dried, the laboratory analysis
can indicate whether psilocybin and/or psilocin are present. The listed laboratories cannot do chemical tests to
confirm the presence of amatoxins or phallotoxins.

Stages of Development of an *Amanita* Mushroom

Breaking of Universal Veil

  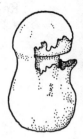

Amanita Button Stages

Patch (Wart) Remnants
of the Universal Veil

Becomes
Annulus

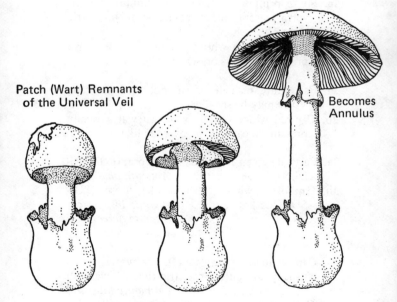

Partial Veil Breaks
Away from the Margin

Botanical Classification
and
Key of Macroscopic Characteristics

Families	Genera
Amanitaceae	*Amanita*
Bolbitiaceae	*Conocybe*
Cortinariaceae	*Gymnopilus*
Coprinaceae	*Panaeolina*
	Panaeolus
Strophariaceae	*Psilocybe*

1a. Spore print white; gills free; annulus present; volva present, either sac-like or in concentric rings **2**

1b. Spore print not white; gills not free; no volva present; annulus present or absent **5**

2a. Cap white or pale green; no warts on cap; Volva may be sac-like **3**

2b. Cap red, white, yellow, or brown; warts usually present on cap; volva never sac-like **4**

3a. Cap pale green; volva sac-like, loose; (POISONOUS) . . . . *Amanita phalloides*

3b. Cap often white; volva sac-like, loose; (POISONOUS). . . . .*Amanita bisporigera*
Amanita ocreata
Amanita verna

4a. Cap yellow, orange to red, or white; warts usually present; concentric rings above bulb . . . . *Amanita muscaria*

4b. Cap brown; warts usually present; rolled lips where bulb and stem meet . . . .
. . . .*Amanita pantherina*

5a. Base of stem bluish; spore print rusty brown or ochraceous **6**

5b. Base of stem not bluish; spore print black, purple, purple brown, lavender gray, rusty orange, or rusty brown **7**

6a. Spore print ochraceous; cap conical, often umbonate. . . . . *Conocybe smithii*

6b. Spore print rusty brown; cap convex, never umbonate . . . . *Conocybe cyanopus*

7a. Spore print rusty orange, or rusty brown **8**

7b. Spore print black, purplish, purple brown, or lavender gray **9**

8a. Spore print rusty brown; annulus present or rudimentary (POISONOUS) *Galerina* species *Conocybe filaris*

8b. Spore print rusty orange; fruiting bodies generally robust; all one color; cespitose; on wood; taste bitter. . .*Gymnopilus spectabilis*

9a. Spore print dark purple brown; not on dung; usually in grass; hygrophanous; white mycelium at base of stem *Panaeolina foenisecii*

9b. Spore print black, purplish, purple brown, or lavender gray **10**

10a. Spore print black; chestnut-colored gills; gregarious. . . . . . . *Panaeolus castaneifolius*

10b. Spore print black, purplish, purple brown, or lavender gray; gills not chestnut-colored **11**

11a. Spore print black. . . . . (Panaeolus) . **12**

11b. Spore print purplish, purple brown, or lavender gray . . . . (Psilocybe) . **17**

12a. Margin appendiculate; usually on dung **13**

12b. Margin not appendiculate; either on dung or not. **14**

13a. Cap hemispherical; often cracking . . .
        . . . . *Panaeolus papilionaceus*
13b. Cap with reticulations . . .*Panaeolus retirugis*
13c. Cap never fully expanding. . .
        . . . . *Panaeolus campanulatus**
        . . . . *Panaeolus sphinctrinus**

14a. Cap and stem pallid or white. **15**
14b. Cap and stem brown or some shade thereof,
    often hygrophanous (darker when wet) **16**

15a. Stem with annulus; cap tall conic, viscid in
    wet weather . . . . *Panaeolus semiovatus*
15b. Cap large; no annulus present . . .
        . . . . *Panaeolus phalaenarum*

16a. White mycelium at base; often cespitose; stem
    somewhat cartilaginous . . .
        . . . *Panaeolus subbalteatus*
16b. Solitary on dung; margin translucent striate
    when moist . . . .*Panaeolus fimicola*
16c. Not visibly on dung; margin also translucent
    striate when moist . . .*Panaeolus acuminatus*

17a. Spore print purple brown; on dung. **18**
17b. Spore print purplish or lavender gray; rarely
    or never on dung **19**

18a. Size small; no annulus present; . . .
        . . . *Psilocybe coprophila*
18b. Size large, annulus conspicuous; non-native
    to the West, often cultivated. . .
        . . . . *Psilocybe cubensis*

19a. Habitat usually in forests (conifer) or forest
    edge; margin not incurved in young fruiting
    bodies . . . . *Psilocybe pelliculosa*

*These two species are very close macroscopically and can only be separated on microscopic characteristics.

19b. Habitat not in forests; usually in pastures, lawns, gardens, mulch, etc.; margin of young caps incurved **20**

20a. Spore print purplish **21**
20b. Spore print lavender gray **22**

21a. Annulus present; stem brown; cap striate and brittle; hygrophanous; often on bark or wood chips . . . . *Psilocybe stuntzii*
21b. No annulus; stem white; in pastures and non-domestic grassy areas *Psilocybe semilanceata*
21c. No annulus; cortina somewhat persistent in young stages; margin may uplift; habit tall; gregarious . . . . *Psilocybe strictipes*

22a. Margin uplifted, often wavy; cortina persistent; spore print dark lavender gray . . .
. . . . *Psilocybe cyanescens*
22b. Margin not uplifted, but often undulating; stem often sinuous; cortina not persistent; spore print light lavender gray . . .
. . . . *Psilocybe baeocystis*

Genus and Species Information

AMANITA

This genus represents a large part of the mushroom flora of North America. *Amanita muscaria* and *A. pantherina* are among the most common. The major fruiting period takes place in the fall, but they can be found growing year round when growing conditions are favorable. The majority of the *Amanitas* are found in forests. The genus is widely distributed in the United States, Canada and Mexico.

Amanitas have four common distinguishing characteristics that are fairly obvious. These are free gills, volva, annulus and a white spore print. The sac-like volva will identify the poisonous species. The mushrooms should be dug up to see the volva accurately.

Poisonous *Amanitas*

The deadly poisonous western members of this genus all share a characteristic not found in *A. muscaria* and *A. pantherina*. This is the sac-like volva. All have an annulus, free gills and a white spore print.

A. bisporigera, *A. ocreata* and *A. verna* are all poisonous. The fruiting bodies are all white. The cap of *A. phalloides* is a pale green or dull yellow with a darker disc. These are the known western deadly *Amanitas*.

Amanita muscaria (Fly Agaric)

This species is the most documented of all mushrooms. The Fly Agaric has a history of use by cultures that may date back thousands of years.

The West has all three color varieties. Red is most abundant on the coast, yellow in the mountains, and the white one is rare but consistently found each year. This common species forms a symbiotic relationship with certain types of trees, mainly pine, spruce, and birch.

The quantity of active substances may vary from location to location and even year to year. The active substances are ibotenic acid, muscimol, and small amounts of muscarine.

Amanita pantherina (Panther Mushroom)

The main distinguishing characteristic for this species is the rolled lip where the stem and bulb meet. Most abundant in Washington, it is widely distributed in North America. The range for *A. pantherina* and *A. muscaria* are the same and they both depend on tree roots for survival. This species fruits well in the spring and continues into the winter in Oregon and Washington.

This mushroom may hybridize with *A. gemmata* (same as *A. junquillea*) causing variable amounts of active substances. It is believed that the darker the cap, the more potent it is. One death in North America has been attributed to the ingestion of this species. Chemical analysis shows the variable presence of ibotenic acid, muscimol and small amounts of muscarine. It should be considered more potent than *A. muscaria.*

(1) *Amanita muscaria* (L. ex Fr.) Hooker
(Fly Agaric)

Spore Print		white
Fruiting Cycle & Range		fall to winter in California, north to Alaska and east to Colorado
Habit & Habitat		solitary to scattered under conifers and in mixed woods
Cap:	*Size*	6–24 cm.
	Shape	globose to convex and plane as it ages
	Color	red, white or yellow and intergrades
	Surface	nearly covered with white warts resulting from the remains of the universal veil; warts can be washed off
	Margin	striate upwards for 1 cm.
	Consistency	fleshy and tough.
Stem:	*Size*	8–25 cm. long, 1–3 cm. thick
	Shape	straight, increasing in size towards the base
	Color	white, may have yellow highlights
	Surface	ragged scales near the base, viscid in wet weather, superior hanging annulus
	Apex	white
	Base	ovate base with concentric scales
	Consistency	solid and firm
Gills:	*Color*	white
	Attachment	free
	Edge	minutely hairy
	Spacing	crowded

Amanita muscaria
(one-half natural size)

(2) *Amanita pantherina* (D.C. ex Fr.) Secr.
(Panther mushroom)

Spore Print		white
Fruiting Cycle & Range		fall to spring in California, north to Alaska and east to Colorado
Habit & Habitat		solitary to scattered under conifers, in mixed woods.
Cap:	*Size*	5–13 cm.
	Shape	globose to convex and plane as it ages
	Color	dark brown, yellowish towards the margin
	Surface	smooth, viscid in wet weather, white pointed warts are the remains of the universal veil; warts can be washed off
	Margin	striate upwards for 1 cm., may have patches of universal veil adhering to it
	Consistency	firm and tough
Stem:	*Size*	5–13 cm. long, 1–3 cm. thick
	Shape	straight and slightly increasing in size towards the base
	Color	white
	Surface	smooth above annulus, superior hanging annulus adheres obliquely
	Apex	white
	Base	ovate base, has a rolled lip where stem and bulb meet, may have ring just above the bulb with a common center
	Consistency	solid and firm, may become hollow as it ages
Gills:	*Color*	shiny white
	Attachment	free
	Edge	finely scalloped
	Spacing	close to crowded

Amanita pantherina
(2) *(one-half natural size)*

CONOCYBE

This genus contains two confirmed psychoactive and at least one poisonous species. The mushrooms are very small and have a rusty brown to ochraceous spore print. The caps are hygrophanous.

Conocybe filaris (Poisonous Species)

This small conifer forest and lawn mushroom has a slightly enlarged base and a hygrophanous cap. The margin of the cap is striate and the stem has a superior annulus. The annulus may disappear or become movable, either up or down the stem. The mushroom is very small and fragile. Known western distribution is in California, Oregon, Washington and Colorado.

Chemical tests in 1974 showed the presence of amatoxins. Pharmacological test results resemble those of *Galerina marginata*. Large fruitings have been observed.

Conocybe cyanopus

This small mushroom grows in lawns and can be distinguished by the blue green coloration at the base of the stem. The white silky stem is similar to *Conocybe coprophila*, a dung inhabiting species of unknown chemical properties.

The base of this species is a deep blue green. This coloration is probably due to the presence of psilocybin. Chemical analysis has shown psilocybin to be present but not psilocin. The potency is believed to be weak and it can be considered a rare species.

Conocybe smithii

This species was once called *Galera cyanopes.* It is the smallest of the known psychoactive mushrooms. It is very fragile and always grows on moss. The lower portion of the stem is slightly enlarged and tinted greenish gray or grayish blue. Considered a rare mushroom in the West, it has been found only in Washington. The presence of psilocybin has been reported but not psilocin. The potency has not been established, but it is suspected to be moderate.

(3) *Conocybe cyanopus* (Atk.) Kühner

Spore Print:		rusty brown
Fruiting Cycle & Range		late summer and early fall, reported only from Washington and Colorado
Habit & Habitat		solitary to gregarious on lawns
Cap:	*Size*	8-12 mm.
	Shape	convex, slightly expanding but not umbonate
	Color	dark brown to almost umber
	Surface	slightly wrinkled
	Margin	minutely striate, may have fragments of veil when young
	Consistency	thin and fragile
Stem:	*Size*	2-4 cm. long, 1-1.5 mm. thick
	Shape	straight and equal
	Color	white
	Surface	silky striate, no veil remnants
	Apex	grayish then brownish streaked as it ages
	Base	deep blue green
	Consistency	fragile
Gills:	*Color*	dull rusty brown
	Attachment	adnate
	Edge	white with a cottony substance on the surface
	Spacing	subclose

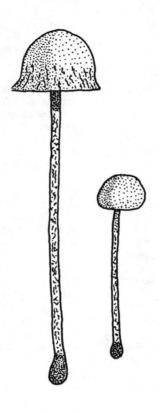

③ Conocybe cyanopus
(twice natural size)

(4) *Conocybe smithii* Watling

Spore Print		ochraceous
Fruiting Cycle & Range		spring to fall, not common and only reported in Washington in the West
Habit & Habitat		scattered on moss under moist conditions
Cap:	*Size*	3–10 mm.
	Shape	obtusely conic, then as it ages the margin expands, umbonate
	Color	hygrophanous, dull brownish yellow, drying to tan buff and glistening
	Surface	striate from the margin to over half way up with radial lines
	Margin	striate when moist
	Consistency	thin and fragile
Stem:	*Size*	1–5 cm. long, 1 mm. thick, 1.5 mm. at base
	Shape	straight and equal
	Color	white then watery white, and finally with a yellowish tint
	Surface	smooth or with faint soft downy hairs, no veil remnants
	Apex	faint, soft downy hairs
	Base	slightly swollen and tinged greenish gray or grayish blue
	Consistency	hollow, fragile and watery.
Gills:	*Color*	creamy yellow then cinnamon rust
	Attachment	adnate
	Edge	minute cottony substance on the surface
	Spacing	subdistant

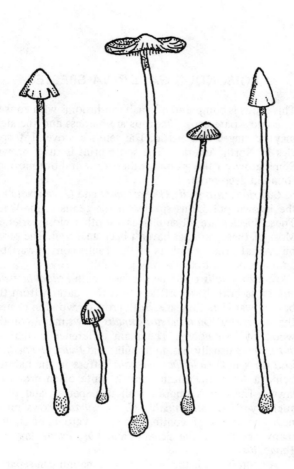

(4) **Conocybe smithii**
(twice natural size)

POISONOUS *GALERINA* SPECIES

This genus is composed of small mushrooms with convex to conic striate caps. The caps are hairless and the stem may be ringed and brittle. The genus has over 150 species in North America. The spore print is rusty brown. Some grow on the ground, others on wood but most are found in deep moss.

Galerina autumnalis, G. marginata and *G. venenata* are the known poisonous species of the genus in the West. These species are all similar as are other close varieties. Most of these varieties haven't been analyzed. The possibility that other members of this genus contain variable amounts of amatoxins is very probable.

G. autumnalis could be confused with *Psilocybe pelliculosa* as both have brittle stems that darken from the base upwards as they age. Both grow on wood in or near the forest, but *Galerina autumnalis* grows mainly on the wood of hardwoods. The main difference is that *G. autumnalis* usually has an annulus and *Psilocybe pelliculosa* does not. *Galerina venenata* differs in the habitat, being a terrestrial mushroom; it quite often grows on lawns. The cap is smooth with this species, and often sticky with *G. autumnalis*. *G. marginata* grows on or near the wood of conifers and is hygrophanous, like many species of the genera *Psilocybe, Panaeolina* and *Panaeolus*.

A spore print is the best way an amateur can separate the poisonous rusty brown spored *Galerinas* from other genera.

GYMNOPILUS

This genus has 73 species in North America. All have a central stem and grow on wood. The colors of the fruiting bodies range from orange brown to red brown and the spores are a bright rusty orange.

Gymnopilus spectabilis

This mushroom has a very bitter taste. The fruiting bodies are concolorous, or all the same color. Also known as *Pholiota spectabilis,* it is quite common in the United States. The rusty orange spore print of this species could be confused with the rusty brown spore print of the deadly genus *Galerina.* The large size of *Gymnopilus spectabilis* will separate the genera.

The western species that have been analyzed have so far not been proved to be psychoactive. European species are also either latent or inactive. East coast and Japanese species are psychoactive. Recent research at the University of Washington has established the presence of bis-noryangonin. This compound is an analog of yangonin, a weak psychoactive substance found in Kava Kava *(Piper methysticum).* It is not known if bis-noryangonin is psychoactive, but it is doubtful since it occurs in edible species. The analysis was done on western species, which haven't been reported as psychoactive. So the active principle remains unknown.

(5) *Gymnopilus spectabilis* (Fr.) A.H. Smith

Spore Print		rusty orange
Fruiting Cycle & Range		fall to winter in California, Oregon, Washington and Idaho
Habit & Habitat		cespitose on alive, dead or buried hardwoods and conifers
Cap:	*Size*	6–18 cm.
	Shape	convex becoming plane as it ages
	Color	buff yellow when young to yellow orange as it ages
	Surface	dry, smooth at first then finely haired as it ages
	Margin	even, no veil remnants
	Consistency	thick and firm
Stem:	*Size*	3–20 cm. long, 8–20 mm. thick or more
	Shape	club shaped or bulbous
	Color	same as cap, sometimes darkening brown near the base, veil pale yellow, leaving a superior fibrillose zone darkening from falling spores
	Surface	smooth, scattered hairs only at maturity
	Apex	concolorous
	Base	pointed or bulbous
	Consistency	solid and firm
Gills:	*Color*	concolorous
	Attachment	adnate to decurrent
	Edge	minutely fringed
	Spacing	crowded to close

⑤ Gymnopilus spectabilis
(one-third natural size)

PANAEOLINA

This genus presently has one species. The genus is very close to the genera *Panaeolus* and *Psathyrella*. Some of the older literature even refers to the member species as a *Psilocybe*. Mycologists can't agree on which genus to put it in. The genus *Panaeolina* is an intermediate. The species of the genus can be separately identified from *Agaricus,* which has free gills, and *Stropharia,* which often has a viscid cap and stem. With the exception of *Panaeolus castaneifolius* the genus *Panaeolus* has smooth spores, unlike *Panaeolina* and some *Psathyrella* species. *Psathyrella* often grows on wood, mosses, straw, sand and sometimes dung. *Panaeolina* grows in grass and not on wood or dung. The dark purple brown spore print differs from a *Galerina* spore print which is rusty brown.

Panaeolina foenisecii (Haymaker's Mushroom)

The Haymaker's mushroom is one of the most common lawn mushrooms in North America. This species is also known as a *Panaeolus* or a *Psathyrella.* Like the latter it has a dark purplish brown spore print. *Panaeolus subbalteatus* looks very similar but has a black spore print.

The stem is rarely flattened like some species of the deadly genus *Galerina.* At the bottom of the stem there will be a mass of white mycelium. Often the stem will be twisted striate and spores may dot the top of the stem as it ages.

Analysis shows this species to be latent and often containing psilocybin and psilocin. Western analysis has often shown the presence of psilocybin (but not psilocin) in small amounts only.

⑥ *Panaeolina foenisecii* (Pers. ex Fr.) Maire

Spore Print		dark purple brown
Fruiting Cycle & Range		late spring to fall, very common throughout the West
Habit & Habitat		solitary to gregarious, grows on lawns and pasture land
Cap:	*Size*	1–4 cm.
	Shape	conic to convex, some will become broadly umbonate to plane, like a sombrero
	Color	hygrophanous, reddish brown drying to dingy buff and shining
	Surface	smooth, may be cracked as it ages or in drying
	Margin	striate when moist, no veil remnants
	Consistency	fleshy
Stem:	*Size*	4–8 cm. long, 1.5–3.5 mm. thick
	Shape	straight and equal or may be flattened
	Color	reddish blond, lighter near the top when young
	Surface	covered with soft, short hairs, sometimes twisted striate; no veil remnants
	Apex	striate
	Base	not enlarged, covered with white mycelium
	Consistency	hollow and rigid
Gills:	*Color*	purple brown to chocolate brown, mottled by maturing spores, then darkening as it ages
	Attachment	adnate
	Edge	even and white
	Spacing	close to subdistant

6 Panaeolina foenisecii
(natural size)

PANAEOLUS

The genus *Panaeolus* is among the most common of the dung inhabiting mushrooms. This genus is probably the first one to be encountered when searching in pastures and other grassy places where horses and cows are kept or have been kept in recent years. Species in this genus are easy to find but sometimes difficult to separate both macroscopically and microscopically.

The color of the spore print is black, and the spores retain their color in concentrated sulphuric acid. All species have caps whose margins overlap the gills. They have central stems that are hollow except for *P. phalaenarum* and often *P. semiovatus.* The gills do not deliquesce (melt away) as in the macroscopically close, black-spored genus *Coprinus.* The gill surfaces, as the mushrooms age, are marked with a variety of intermingled colors. This condition is called variegated or mottled. The edge of the gill is normally white. Some species of *Psathyrella* also exhibit these phenomena, but unlike *Panaeolus* most are very fragile and typically have a purple cast in a spore print.

The genus can be separated into three groups. The first group often has remnants on the margin, a product of the partial veil. This group is composed of *P. campanulatus, P. papilionaceus, P. retirugis, and P. sphinctrinus.* The second group lacks the remnants on the margin. It has four members: *P. castaneifolius, P. acuminatus, P. fimicola,* and *P. subbalteatus.* The first member of the second group is never on dung, the second is seldom seen in dung. The third member is always solitary and the last is often cespitose. The last three members may have zoning on the cap with the last species being more consistent.

The third group has a whitish coloration on the stem and cap. The two members in this group are *P. phalaenarum* and *P. semiovatus.*

Most of the *Panaeolus* species in this book usually grow on horse or cow dung. Some of these mushrooms grow on fairly fresh manure, and some grow on dung that is in an advanced state of decomposition. Little is known about this ecological succession.

The *Panaeolus* species that stain blue are not found in the West with the exception of one white, undescribed species. The other species that stain blue are *P. cyanescens, P. cambodginiensis,* and *P. tropicalis.* The blueing, as in the *Psilocybe* species, is likely due to the occurrence of psilocybin. *Panaeolus cyanescens* and *P. tropicalis* are found in Hawaii. *P. ater,* an active species, may have been found in Alaska recently. The species of this genus consistently contain unidentified factors. These unidentified factors may or may not be mildly psychoactive. Some species do contain psilocybin and/or psilocin. Most species are latent, that is they have the potential to be psychoactive.

Panaeolus acuminatus

Only recently reported from Washington, this mushroom is quite common along the west coast. It is not always found on dung, at least visibly, and can be easily identified by its translucent striate margin in wet weather. The cap typically is pointed when young, opening as it ages, with the width becoming greater than the height. The presence of active substances has not yet been verified, but the chances are quite good that some strains do contain psilocybin and/or psilocin.

Panaeolus campanulatus

This is a very common and widely distributed species in the United States. The toothlike margin is a fairly constant identification characteristic with young mushrooms. Sometimes found growing in beds of cultivated mushrooms, this mushroom grows on manure and can be easily cultivated in a moist chamber on sterilized horse dung. In this medium, at normal room temperature, it will go through the whole spore cycle in five weeks. One fruiting body can produce over 200 million spores.

Chemical analysis consistently shows the presence of unidentified factors. The psychoactive potential of this species has been well documented for a long time. Analysis of species from California and Oregon has confirmed the presence of psilocybin. Other locations are sure to be found as more strains are tested.

Panaeolus castaneifolius

This species is also known as a *Psathyrella* and was previously reported in Washington in the West. I have found it on the Oregon coast. This species is not as rare on the east coast.

Some have reported this species to have a strong odor and an unpleasant taste. This was not the case with those found in Oregon. This rare species always grows gregarious and always grows around grass. Macroscopically it is similar to *Panaeolina foenisecii* but has black spores and the gill colors are different. Microscopically they are also very similar, as both have warted spores. *Panaeolus castaneifolius* should be in the genus *Panaeolina* because of the latter characteristic.

This latent species has been found to contain psilocin. This was not the case of those from Oregon. No potency has been established.

Panaeolus fimicola

This species was first found on the west coast in 1876, in California. It might be considered a rare western mushroom but not as rare in the eastern United

States. The *Panaeolus* species receive little attention by mycologists since they are somewhat difficult to separate, and there are so many larger mushrooms of greater interest. So it may not be as rare as indicated—it may have just been overlooked.

The scalloped margin, zoning on the cap and the solitary habit are the main distinguishing characteristics. *P. subbalteatus,* as it ages, takes on a similar zoning of the cap.

Chemical analysis by Ola'h in 1969 shows this to be a latent species sometimes containing psilocybin and psilocin. The potency has not been established. It may, like other *Panaeolus* species, contain unidentified factors.

Panaeolus papilionaceus

This species has been reportedly used as a mind altering agent in Central America along with *P. sphinctrinus.* This mushroom sometimes grows with cultivated species and looks very similar to *P. campanulatus.* Some mycologists consider them to be the same. The cracking on the cap is the main identification characteristic along with the hemispherical cap. *P. campanulatus* and *Panaeolina foenisecii* may also crack in a similar fashion, but not as commonly.

Analysis of western species shows the presence of unidentified factors. The presence of psilocybin and/or psilocin has not been established. The potency has also not been established. It can be considered rare in the West.

Panaeolus phalaenarum

This mushroom can be easily separated from the other species of *Panaeolus* by its large size and solid stem. Like *P. semiovatus* it has the white coloration not found in the other known species of *Panaeolus* of the West.

It is only suspected to have psychoactive strains. Chemical analysis is lacking but in view of its close relationship to the genus, there is a possibility that it has active strains.

Panaeolus retirugis

This mushroom looks similar to *Panaeolus campanulatus, P. papilionaceus,* and *P. sphinctrinus,* but can be distinguished by the raised ribs on the cap. The veil in young fruiting bodies breaks into v-shaped loops that cling to the margin of the cap. The size will vary according to the environment, being larger in moist soil and wet weather, and smaller in dry soil and dry weather. The older name for this species is *P. carbonarius.*

Western analysis of this latent species has shown the presence of psilocybin and unidentified factors.

Panaeolus semiovatus

This is the only *Panaeolus* in the West with a persistent annulus and a viscid cap. For these reasons some authors have placed it in a separate genus and called it *Anellaria semiovata.* It is one of the most common *Panaeolus* species from central Oregon east to Denver, Colorado. Chemical analysis has shown the presence of psilocybin only in collections from Colorado.

Panaeolus sphinctrinus

Even the mycologists who specialize in this genus have a difficult time separating this species from *P. campanulatus.* The true *P. sphinctrinus,* as the name implies, remains in a natural state of contraction. The margin of the young mushrooms may be appressed to the stem and give the appearance of a white collar before it breaks up.

Chemical analysis of this latent species has shown the presence of psilocybin and/or psilocin. Many strains tested were inactive or active in small concentrations. This species appears to have more active strains than *P. campanulatus.*

Panaeolus subbalteatus

This mushroom has also been known as *P. rufus* and *P. venenosus.* But *P. rufus* tastes like fresh meal, and *P. subbalteatus* tastes like commercial mushrooms. Venenosus means poisonous, and the species was so named because of its psychoactive reputation. The zoning on the cap is the most noticeable characteristic. *Panaeolina foenisecii* looks most like this species and a spore print will separate the two. Both have white mycelium at the bottom of the stem. The stem often stains brown—this may actually be a blueing reaction that is hidden by the brown coloration of the stem. Blueing may sometimes be noticed in the mycelium.

This is the most consistently psychoactive *Panaeolus* of the West. It is also one of the most common, and easiest to grow. The potency is low and equal to *Psilocybe stuntzii* on a dry weight basis. Chemical analysis consistently shows psilocybin and sometimes psilocin.

⑦ *Panaeolus acuminatus* (Schaeff.) Fr.

Spore Print		black
Fruiting Cycle & Range		all year except late winter—northern California to northern Washington
Habit & Habitat		solitary to gregarious, sometimes on well manured earth
Cap:	*Size*	15 mm.–30 mm.
	Shape	conical then expanding, wider than high with age
	Color	hygrophanous, dark brown drying to tan brown and shiny
	Surface	smooth
	Margin	scalloped when young and translucent striate when moist
	Consistency	fleshy
Stem:	*Size*	25–75 mm. long, 2–4 mm. thick
	Shape	straight and equal
	Color	pallid above, brown downwards—all brown with age
	Surface	smooth, covered with a white powder
	Apex	striate
	Base	enlarged and covered with white mycelium
	Consistency	hollow and brittle
Gills:	*Color*	pallid, blackening as it ages
	Attachment	adnexed
	Edge	white
	Spacing	crowded

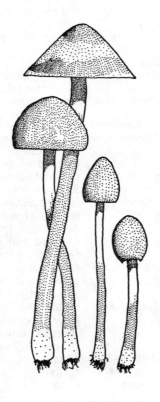

Panaeolus acuminatus
(natural size)

(8) *Panaeolus campanulatus* (Bull. ex. Fr.) Quél.

Spore Print		black
Fruiting Cycle & Range		spring to winter from southern California north to Alaska and east to Colorado
Habit & Habitat		solitary to gregarious on dung in pasture lands or manured soil
Cap:	*Size*	1–4 cm.
	Shape	obtuse, parabolic to campanulate, never expanded
	Color	hygrophanous, gray brown drying yellow gray brown
	Surface	smooth, may crack as it ages
	Margin	incurved when young, then expanding, veil is white toothed fringe, appendiculate
	Consistency	thin and brittle
Stem:	*Size*	3–12 cm. long, 1–3 mm. thick
	Shape	straight and equal
	Color	reddish brown, the top often dotted with spores
	Surface	polished and covered with a fine white powder
	Apex	substriate
	Base	covered with white mycelium and slightly enlarged
	Consistency	hollow and fragile
Gills:	*Color*	gray becoming mottled as spores mature, then darkening to purple brown as it ages
	Attachment	adnate
	Edge	white
	Spacing	close

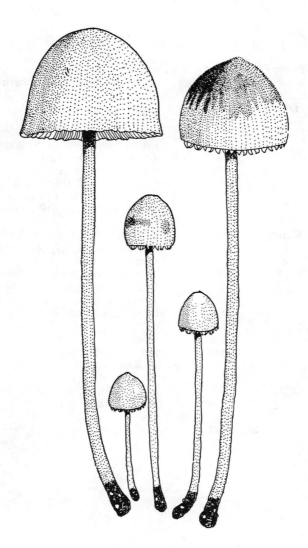

(8) **Panaeolus campanulatus**
(natural size)

(9) *Panaeolus castaneifolius* (Murr.) Ola'h

Spore Print		black
Fruiting Cycle & Range		summer to fall, very rare in Washington and Oregon
Habit & Habitat		gregarious in grassy places
Cap:	*Size*	1–4 cm.
	Shape	convex, never fully expanding
	Color	hygrophanous, dark cinnamon drying to pinkish buff
	Surface	smooth, often wrinkled
	Margin	even and incurved when young, no veil remnants, translucent striate when moist
	Consistency	thick and firm
Stem:	*Size*	4.5–7 cm. long, 4–6 mm. thick
	Shape	straight and slightly tapering toward the base
	Color	same color as cap but may be lighter near the top when young
	Surface	finely powdered, no veil remnants
	Apex	striate
	Base	not enlarged
	Consistency	hollow, cartilaginous, thick and firm
Gills:	*Color*	chestnut, darkening as it ages
	Attachment	adnate to adnexed
	Edge	white
	Spacing	subclose

⑨ Panaeolus castaneifolius
(natural size)

(10)   *Panaeolus fimicola* (Fr.) Quél.

Spore Print		black
Fruiting Cycle & Range		spring to mid-fall in California and probably Idaho
Habit & Habitat		solitary on dung
Cap:	*Size*	1–4 cm.
	Shape	campanulate to convex
	Color	when moist, brownish gray, drying to yellowish gray; encircling brown ring near the margin, sometimes with a lighter ring within, darker when wet
	Surface	smooth
	Margin	scalloped
	Consistency	thin and brittle
Stem:	*Size*	5–10 cm. long, 2–4 mm. thick
	Shape	straight and equal
	Color	dingy white, lighter at the top, brown as it ages
	Surface	smooth, the top half covered with a white powder, spores may dot the top of the stem
	Apex	striate
	Base	somewhat enlarged
	Consistency	hollow, soft and fragile
Gills:	*Color*	gray, becoming mottled and darkening as spores mature
	Attachment	adnate
	Edge	white
	Spacing	close

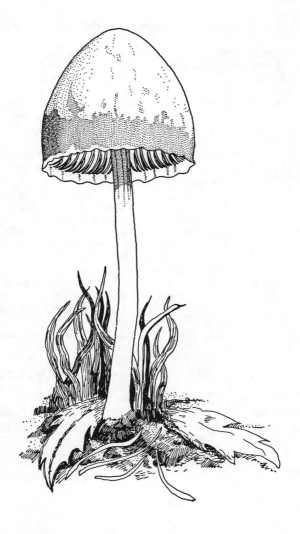

10 **Panaeolus fimicola**
(natural size)

(11) *Panaeolus papilionaceus* (Bull. ex Fr.) Quél.

Spore Print		black
Fruiting Cycle & Range		spring to fall in northern and southern California, Oregon, and Washington
Habit & Habitat		solitary to gregarious on the ground in decomposing dung, pastures and manured lawns
Cap:	*Size*	2–4 cm.
	Shape	campanulate or hemispherical then slightly more open
	Color	pale gray, as it ages tinged with pink, darker near the top and shiny when dry
	Surface	smooth or cracked
	Margin	extending over the gills, may have veil remnants, appendiculate
	Consistency	thin, brittle
Stem:	*Size*	5-7 cm. long, 3-6 mm. thick
	Shape	straight and equal
	Color	whitish, darkening brown as it ages
	Surface	smooth, shiny, covered with a fine white powder
	Apex	striate
	Base	brownish, may be somewhat enlarged
	Consistency	hollow, stiff
Gills:	*Color*	whitish, becoming mottled then blackening with age
	Attachment	adnate
	Edge	white
	Spacing	close

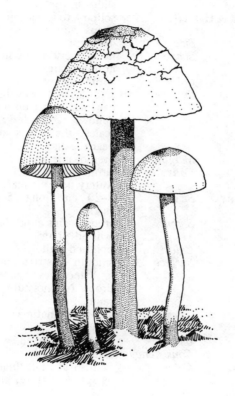

(11) **Panaeolus papilionaceus**
(natural size)

12 *Panaeolus phalaenarum* (Fr.) Quél.

Spore Print		black
Fruiting Cycle & Range		spring to fall in California, Washington, Alaska, and possibly Oregon
Habit & Habitat		solitary to gregarious on dung heaps and manured ground
Cap:	*Size*	4-10 cm.
	Shape	hemispherical to convex, never umbonate
	Color	white when young
	Surface	smooth, as it ages the whitish cap may break up into dingy yellow, rather large angular scales, the scales are larger near the disc
	Margin	even or uneven
	Consistency	firm, rather thick, may be watery near the margin
Stem:	*Size*	8-20 cm. long, 5-15 mm. thick
	Shape	straight and equal or may be twisted striate
	Color	polished white
	Surface	smooth or striate, upper part is sometimes beaded with drops of moisture, no veil remnants
	Apex	striate, sometimes extending down the stem
	Base	straight or curved
	Consistency	solid and tough
Gills.	*Color*	whitish at first, then mottled as spores mature, black as it ages
	Attachment	adnate
	Edge	white with a cottony substance on the surface
	Spacing	close

(12) Panaeolus phalaenarum
(one-half natural size)

Panaeolus retirugis (Fr.) Gill.

Spore Print		black
Fruiting Cycle & Range		spring to fall in northern and southern California, Oregon and Washington
Habit & Habitat		solitary to gregarious in pastures and manured grassy areas
Cap:	*Size*	1–3 cm.
	Shape	globose, conic or campanulate
	Color	dark smoky becoming gray brown as it ages; darker when moist, shiny when dry
	Surface	reticulate with raised ribs or wrinkled
	Margin	incurved when young, appressed to the stem, fragments from the ringlike veil may be attached, appendiculate
	Consistency	thin and fragile
Stem:	*Size*	5–9 cm. long, 2–4 mm. thick
	Shape	straight and equal
	Color	whitish becoming purplish as it ages, darkest near the base
	Surface	polished and finely powdered, no veil remnants
	Apex	striate
	Base	darker, may be slightly enlarged
	Consistency	hollow, stiff and fragile
Gills:	*Color*	white then mottled becoming black as it ages
	Attachment	adnate or adnexed
	Edge	white and downy
	Spacing	close

13 **Panaeolus retirugis**
(natural size)

(14)

Panaeolus semiovatus
(Sow. ex Fr.) Lundell & Nannf.

Spore Print		black
Fruiting Cycle & Range		spring to fall in California, Oregon, Idaho, Washington, Alaska and Colorado
Habit & Habitat		solitary to gregarious on dung
Cap:	*Size*	2-6 cm.
	Shape	tall conic to campanulate or parabolic
	Color	clay white, as it ages pallid buff, darker in the shade
	Surface	smooth, when dry may be cracked
	Margin	even, paler, no veil remnants
	Consistency	thin, soft and fragile, viscid in wet weather
Stem:	*Size*	7-15 cm. long, 4-10 mm. thick
	Shape	straight and equal
	Color	whitish
	Surface	smooth, membranous veil, leaving a persistent annulus, darkened by falling spores
	Apex	striate
	Base	slightly enlarged
	Consistency	hollow as it ages
Gills:	*Color*	light becoming mottled, then darkening as it ages
	Attachment	adnate
	Edge	even and minutely fringed, white
	Spacing	close to subdistant

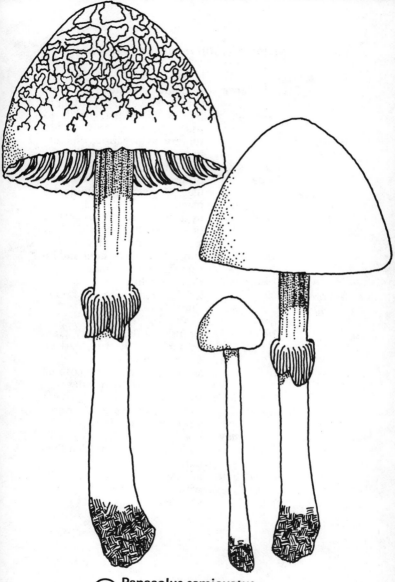

⑭ Panaeolus semiovatus
(natural size)

(15) *Panaeolus sphinctrinus* (Fr.) Quél.

Spore Print		black
Fruiting Cycle & Range		in milder climates may grow year round, major fruiting in fall in California, north to Alaska and east to Colorado
Habit & Habitat		solitary to gregarious on dung in manured gardens and lawns
Cap:	*Size*	1–3 cm.
	Shape	obtuse then broadly campanulate, never expanding to plane
	Color	hygrophanous, brown or dark olive gray drying pallid buff
	Surface	smooth, shiny when dry
	Margin	appressed to the stem and incurved, appendiculate
	Consistency	fleshy and brittle
Stem:	*Size*	2.5–7.5 cm. long, 2–4 mm. thick
	Shape	straight and equal
	Color	whitish to dark smoky gray, lighter near the top, darkening as it ages
	Surface	smooth, polished and covered with a fine white powder
	Apex	substriate
	Base	slightly enlarged and covered with white mycelium
	Consistency	hollow and fragile
Gills:	*Color*	pallid becoming mottled then darkening as it ages
	Attachment	adnate
	Edge	white
	Spacing	crowded

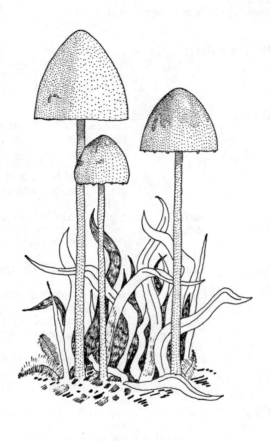

(15) **Panaeolus sphinctrinus**
(natural size)

16 *Panaeolus subbalteatus* (Berk. & Br.) Sacc.

Spore Print		black
Fruiting Cycle & Range		spring to fall in California, Oregon, Washington and Idaho
Habit & Habitat		solitary to gregarious or sometimes cespitose on freshly manured lawns, open ground, has been found with cultivated mushrooms
Cap:	*Size*	2–5 cm.
	Shape	convex or slightly umbonate, can be irregular and even plane
	Color	hygrophanous, dull deep fawn color, marked near the margin with a dark, narrow zone, pallid when dry
	Surface	slightly wrinkled or smooth
	Margin	incurved then expanding, not translucent striate
	Consistency	fleshy
Stem:	*Size*	2–8 cm. long, 2–10 mm. thick
	Shape	straight and equal
	Color	somewhat darker than cap, generally brown
	Surface	smooth, marked with short white fibrils, no veil remnants
	Apex	striate
	Base	not enlarged, covered with white mycelium
	Consistency	hollow, thick and cartilaginous
Gills:	*Color*	brownish, mottled then blackening
	Attachment	adnate or adnexed
	Edge	white and slightly fringed
	Spacing	close

(16) **Panaeolus subbalteatus**
(natural size)

PSILOCYBE

This genus has many species. Just how many hasn't been established yet, as a complete monograph does not yet exist, and new species are still being collected. The blue staining species of this genus are the only ones which have psychoactive properties. The one exception is *Psilocybe coprophila*, which often blues only at the base of the stem in the mycelium. There are at least seven western *Psilocybe* species which are psychoactive.

This group of mushrooms is fairly easy to identify. With the exception of *P. coprophila* and *P. cubensis*, all of the species in this book have a thin translucent pellicle of slimy gelatinous material that can be peeled easily when wet. The pellicle disappears as the mushroom dries. Often these mushrooms will have a bluish or greenish cast. This is not always the case, but frequently happens in the wet or dry state.

The species of this genus included in this book are hygrophanous, again with the exceptions of *P. coprophila* and *P. cubensis*. The hygrophanous mushroom changes color as it loses moisture. The young mushrooms are usually found in the wet state and dry as they age.

The color of the spore print of this genus will be purplish to lavender gray, and purple brown with *P. coprophila* and *P. cubensis*. Other genera with a similar spore color are *Agaricus*, *Stropharia*, *Naematoloma* and *Psathyrella*. *Agaricus* species can be identified by their free gills. *Stropharias* usually have an annulus and stem that are quite often viscid. *Naematoloma* species have a cap that is not hygrophanous. *Psathyrella* species lack the blue colorations that most psychoactive *Psilocybe* species take on when injured or in drying. None of these other genera have a removable pellicle on the cap, with the exception of some *Stropharias*. Still other mushrooms resembling the *Psilocybe* species exist, but they can only be identified by means of a spore print.

The western members of this genus can be separated into four groups. The first group consists of *P. cyanescens, P. baeocystis* and *P. strictipes. P. semilanceata* and *P. stuntzii* constitute the next group and can be found side by side in pastures. The latter species does well by itself in bark and wood chips. The forest inhabiting group consists solely of *P. pelliculosa,* and the dung group has two members: *P. coprophila* and the non-native *P. cubensis.*

Psilocybe baeocystis

This species was first reported in Eugene, Oregon, in 1945. The mushroom described at that time differs from the commonly known species. The margin can be undulated and often resembles the edge of a bottle cap. Often the stem is characterized by bends or folds—apparently this is a product of the habitat. The most constant characteristic is the brown spot in the center of the cap after drying. Blueing usually occurs on the cap and stem, especially with age. This blueing is thought to be a degradation of the active components.

In the fall, it is not uncommon to find 50 or so mushrooms fruiting at once in a small area. Growth mainly takes place on lawns, under ivy, in woodchips and in woodchip and bark mixtures. The landscaped areas of businesses, homes, freeways, and parks often provide a suitable habitat. It will return each fall at the same locations and can be transplanted effectively.

This species, along with *P. cyanescens,* and possibly *P. strictipes,* is the most potent of the western *Psilocybes.* One death, that of a child, was attributed to *P. baeocys-*

tis (at least in part, since there were other mushrooms involved). Analysis shows the variable presence of baeocystin, norbaeocystin, psilocybin, psilocin, and unidentified substances. Baeocystin and norbaeocystin are very close chemically to psilocybin and psilocin. Ingestion of .5 grams dry weight is enough to cause distinct perceptual changes. The degradation of the active substances is somewhat faster than in *P. semilanceata,* and *P. baeocystis* is twice as potent. Mushrooms that contain larger amounts of psilocin will degrade quicker.

Psilocybe coprophila

This species is unlike the other active western *Psilocybes.* It lacks the pellicle, has purple brown spores and grows on dung. It also lacks the blue staining, although blueing has been noticed in the mycelium. Very similar, and also found on dung, is *P. merdaria.* This mushroom has a fibrillose annulus and a lighter cap. Recent analysis has shown low amounts of psilocybin in this species, but this must be verified.

It is only recently that *P. coprophila* has been found to contain low amounts of psilocybin, and only when fresh.

Psilocybe cubensis

This is not a native of the West. It is included here because it is very easy to cultivate and is the most common psychoactive mushroom cultivated in the United States. Growth is very fast. A fruiting body can mature in two days. Different media and cultivation techniques produce larger amounts of psychoactive alkaloids than others. Light is one factor needed for the production of the fruiting bodies, but it is a triggering device and is not associated with chlorophyll.

This species is found on dung, mainly cow dung. It is native to the Southeastern United States, from Texas to Florida and south to Central America. Some authors call it *Stropharia cubensis.*

This mushroom consistently contains psilocybin and/-or psilocin. Ingestion of two or three mushrooms will cause a distinct alteration of consciousness. The potency is considered low for a psychoactive species on a dry weight basis.

Psilocybe cyanescens

The color of the cap is chestnut in the wet state, yellowish to yellowish brown as it dries and ages. In age the margin may lift up and become wavy, and is more pronounced than that of *P. strictipes*. Some species of the deadly genus *Galerina* closely resemble *P. cyanescens*. A spore print will separate the two genera macroscopically.

The habitat of this species is quite variable. It has been observed growing directly out of moss covered stumps (alive with shoots) of Red Elderberry *(Sambucus sp.)* and the Butterfly Bush *(Buddleja sp.);* under Ivy *(Hedera sp.),* in wood chips and bales of straw; and most commonly in tall rank grass. The mycelium is very aggressive and can be transplanted quite effectively.

The distribution ranges west of the Sierra and the Cascade mountain ranges from California north to British Columbia. Chemical analysis shows the variable presence of psilocybin, psilocin and unidentified substances. The potency is strong for a *Psilocybe* species and equal to *P. baeocystis*.

Psilocybe pelliculosa

First reported at Lake Tahkenitch, Oregon in 1935, this mushroom can be found in the forests of the northwest and Northern California. The very similar *P. silvatica* is found from New York to Michigan and north to Canada.

It is very easy to overlook, especially in a dense forest where light is minimal. The margin is not incurved as are the rest of the active *Psilocybe* species in the West (with the exception of *P. coprophila*). The general appearance is very similar to *P. semilanceata* except for the margin and the stem, which darkens from the base up, turning nearly black as it ages. Small roots can often be observed coming out of the base. The base sometimes has forest debris attached to it. Some varieties have a stem that remains white. This phenomenon, and the roots, are believed to be the product of habitat. This species is always found in or near the forest, whereas *P. semilanceata* is found in open fields and pasture lands.

This mushroom and *P. silvatica* are considered by some to be the same. Others believe the latter is a separate eastern species. If not the same, they are certainly very similar. Both consistently contain psilocybin and/or psilocin in low amounts, in addition to unidentified substances. Ingestion will cause consciousness alteration only if more than 40 mushrooms are consumed. Potency is low, normally half that of *P. semilanceata* on a dry weight basis. The psilocybin and psilocin will completely degrade within a year in dried specimens.

Psilocybe semilanceata (Liberty Cap)

Liberty Cap is the common name for this species. The name dates back a long time, and refers to the hat used in the French Revolution. Visually this mushroom looks very much like *P. pelliculosa,* but differs mainly with its incurved margin and white stem. The habitats are also different. The Liberty Cap is most often found around grass roots, and may rely on them somewhat for survival. It is seldom found growing on dung and is not found in the forest. It seldom grows in domestic grassy areas unless planted.

At one time the members of this species that turn blue were considered to be a variety of the ones that remained white. Both types contain psilocybin, psilocin, baeocystin and unidentified substances rather consistently. The potency is moderate and the dried specimens are thought to retain the active substances longer than other *Psilocybes.* Enzymes may be responsible for differing degrees of degradation within the genera of psilocy-bin-and/or-psilocin-containing mushrooms.

Psilocybe strictipes

This mushroom can be distinguished from the other *Psilocybe* species by its subcespitose fruiting habit. It is seldom solitary. It is usually taller than the other *Psilocybe* species and unlike the other closely related species *P. baeocystis* and *P. cyanescens*, it has a greater stem to cap size ratio in mature specimens. This northwest species has so far only been found from Oregon north to British Columbia and is considered rarer than the other members of this group.

Chemical analysis shows the presence of unidentified substances, psilocybin and/or psilocin. The potency of these active substances is thought to be high, equal to that of *P. cyanescens* and *P. baeocystis.*

Psilocybe stuntzii

This species fruits abundantly in Washington where it is the most common *Psilocybe*. It has a persistent annulus, is very fragile, and grows alongside *P. semilanceata* in pastures. This is a newly identified species and the name has only recently been published. Chemical analysis shows the presence of psilocybin and psilocin with the potency equal to that of *P. pelliculosa* in fresh dried specimens.

(17) *Psilocybe baeocystis* Sing. & A.H. Smith

Spore Print		lavender gray
Fruiting Cycle & Range		fall in California, north to British Columbia
Habit & Habitat		solitary to cespitose on peat moss, lawns, wood chips and in flower gardens
Cap:	*Size*	15–50 mm.
	Shape	conic when young to convex or subplane as it ages, umbonate
	Color	hygrophanous, olive brown drying to tan brown with a dark spot in the center, blue tints especially near the margin when bruised or in drying
	Surface	smooth, thin gelatinous pellicle, removable in wet weather, pellicle translucent
	Margin	incurved when young, minutely striate when wet, often undulating, cortina not persistent
	Consistency	pliant to brittle
Stem:	*Size*	4–7 cm. long, 2–4 mm. thick
	Shape	straight and equal or equal to subequal, often sinuous
	Color	whitish, staining blue with age or in bruising, dark brown pith inside
	Surface	composed of fine white fibrils
	Apex	white where gills and stem connect
	Base	enlarged only slightly
	Consistency	cartilaginous and stuffed with loose fibrils
Gills:	*Color*	purple gray, somewhat mottled
	Attachment	adnate to uncinate
	Edge	whitish
	Spacing	subclose

(17) **Psilocybe baeocystis**
(natural size)

⑱ *Psilocybe coprophila* (Bull. ex Fr.) Kummer

Spore Print		purple brown
Fruiting Cycle & Range		spring to early winter, widely distributed in the West
Habit & Habitat		solitary to gregarious on dung
Cap:	*Size*	1–2 cm.
	Shape	convex
	Color	gray brown to dark brown
	Surface	viscid or dry, superficial specks when young
	Margin	smooth, may have fine hairs on margin
	Consistency	thin
Stem:	*Size*	2–6 cm. long, 1–3 mm. thick
	Shape	straight and equal
	Color	yellow brown
	Surface	dry and silky
	Apex	smooth
	Base	enlarged with mycelium
	Consistency	stiff, cartilaginous
Gills:	*Color*	gray brown, dark purple brown as it ages
	Attachment	adnate
	Edge	white
	Spacing	distant

Psilocybe coprophila
(natural size)

19 *Psilocybe cubensis* (Earle) Sing.

Spore Print		purple brown
Fruiting Cycle & Range		spring to midwinter in its natural habitat in the southeastern U.S. and year round when cultivated
Habit & Habitat		solitary to gregarious on cow dung, can be cultivated on compost
Cap:	*Size*	2–8 cm.
	Shape	conic, campanulate to convex or plane as it ages, umbonate
	Color	whitish to pale yellow as it ages and staining dark blue
	Surface	smooth with tiny white specks when young
	Margin	only incurved when young, with collar
	Consistency	firm and fleshy
Stem:	*Size*	4–15 cm. long, 5–15 mm. thick
	Shape	straight and equal or slightly enlarging towards the base
	Color	white staining blue when handled or bruised, blueing may be more pronounced in the cultivated species
	Surface	smooth with a white, superior membranous annulus, darkened by falling spores
	Apex	striate
	Base	may be somewhat enlarged
	Consistency	hollow as it ages
Gills:	*Color*	gray to violet gray and mottled to black as it ages
	Attachment	adnate to adnexed
	Edge	white
	Spacing	close

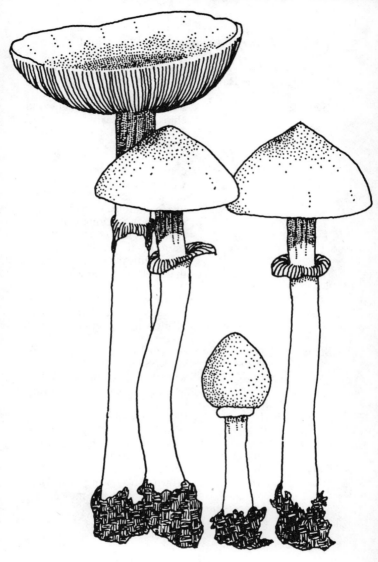

(19) Psilocybe cubensis
(natural size)

Psilocybe cyanescens Wakefield

Spore Print		dark lavender gray
Fruiting Cycle & Range		fall in California, north to British Columbia
Habit & Habitat		solitary to cespitose on wood chips, tall grass, stumps, and dead twigs in pasture lands, rarely in woods
Cap:	*Size*	2–5 cm.
	Shape	convex becoming expanded with age, uplifted, wavy, often with umbo
	Color	hygrophanous, chestnut color when moist, drying yellowish, staining blue where touched
	Surface	smooth, thin gelatinous pellicle, removable in wet weather, pellicle translucent
	Margin	striate when moist, often blue, persistent cortina when young
	Consistency	pliant when young, brittle as it ages
Stem:	*Size*	6–8 cm. long, 2.5–6 mm. thick
	Shape	straight and equal
	Color	whitish, changing to blue when bruised or during drying
	Surface	silky fibrillose
	Apex	slightly flared
	Base	slightly enlarged and may be curved, often with small roots
	Consistency	rigid and cartilaginous
Gills:	*Color*	cinnamon becoming reddish brown as it ages and the spores mature, somewhat mottled
	Attachment	adnate
	Edge	paler
	Spacing	subdistant

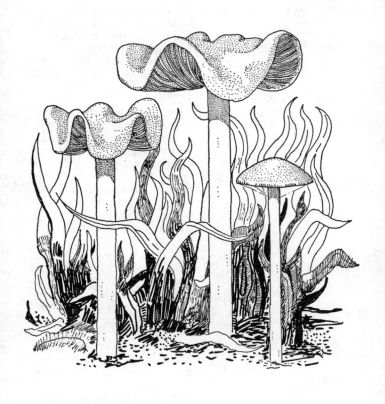

Psilocybe cyanescens
(natural size)

Psilocybe pelliculosa
(A.H. Smith) Sing. & A.H. Smith

Spore Print		purplish
Fruiting Cycle & Range		fall to winter in northern California, Oregon, Washington, Idaho and British Columbia
Habit & Habitat		scattered to gregarious or cespitose on sticks and forest debris in and near conifer forests
Cap:	*Size*	8–25 mm.
	Shape	conic to obtusely campanulate
	Color	hygrophanous, yellow brown to gray brown drying lighter, stains slightly blue when touched or bruised and as it ages
	Surface	smooth, thin gelatinous pellicle, removable in wet weather, pellicle translucent
	Margin	straight, never incurved, continate when young
	Consistency	thin
Stem:	*Size*	4–8 cm. long, 1.5–2.5 mm. thick
	Shape	straight and equal
	Color	pale to brownish below, blackish brown as it ages or remaining white
	Surface	smooth, no veil remnants, fibrillose
	Apex	gills eventually separating from apex
	Base	enlarged with forest debris and white mycelium, may have roots and is often bent
	Consistency	thin and tough, cartilaginous
Gills:	*Color*	cinnamon when young, turning gray brown as spores mature
	Attachment	adnate
	Edge	white or paler
	Spacing	close

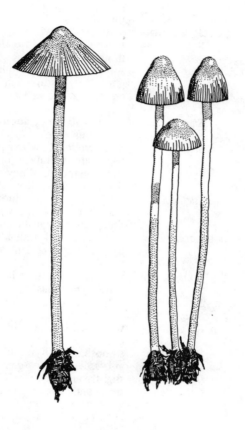

21 Psilocybe pelliculosa
(natural size)

(22) *Psilocybe semilanceata* (Fr. ex Secr.) Kummer
(Liberty Cap)

Spore Print		purplish
Fruiting Cycle & Range		spring to mid-winter from northern California to British Columbia
Habit & Habitat		solitary to gregarious near grass in pasture lands and grassy meadows, rarely on dung
Cap:	*Size*	5 mm.–30 mm., about twice as high as wide
	Shape	mostly conical, with a pointed top, rarely convex or plane
	Color	hygrophanous, dingy brown drying to pale yellow
	Surface	smooth, thin gelatinous pellicle, removable in wet weather, pellicle translucent
	Margin	incurved, black radial lines go up with age, cortinate when young
	Consistency	thin and pliant when wet, brittle as it dries
Stem:	*Size*	3–8 cm. long, 2 mm. thick
	Shape	straight and equal
	Color	whitish, may have blue highlights
	Surface	smooth, no veil remnants
	Apex	gills ascending to apex
	Base	slightly enlarged
	Consistency	thin and tough enough to wrap around your finger, pliant, contains a darker pith inside
Gills:	*Color*	cream colored, then becoming purple black as the spores mature
	Attachment	adnexed
	Edge	white
	Spacing	subclose

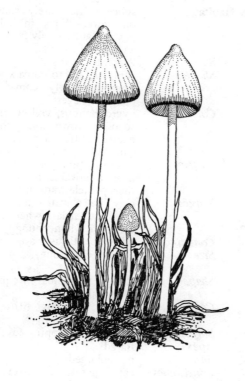

Psilocybe semilanceata
(natural size)

(23) *Psilocybe strictipes* Sing. & A.H. Smith

Spore Print — purplish

Fruiting Cycle & Range — fall in Oregon, Washington and possibly British Columbia

Habit & Habitat — subcespitose, rarely solitary, on wood chips, in soil of pasture lands, rarely in conifer and mixed woods

Cap:

Size	2–5 cm.
Shape	campanulate to convex when young, broadly convex to plane as it ages
Color	hygrophanous, yellow brown to olive brown drying to cinnamon buff, paler near margin, stains blue
Surface	smooth, thin gelatinous pellicle, removable in wet weather, pellicle translucent
Margin	may be elevated and wavy with age, striate when moist, cortinate when young
Consistency	pliant, brittle as it ages

Stem:

Size	10–14 cm. long, 2–4 mm. thick
Shape	straight and equal or equal to subequal
Color	whitish, staining blue and sometimes brown
Surface	pallid from appressed fibrils
Apex	flared
Base	not enlarged
Consistency	cartilaginous and stuffed with a brown pith, sometimes minutely hollow

Gills:

Color	pallid becoming dark chocolate as the spores mature, somewhat mottled
Attachment	adnate
Edge	white
Spacing	close

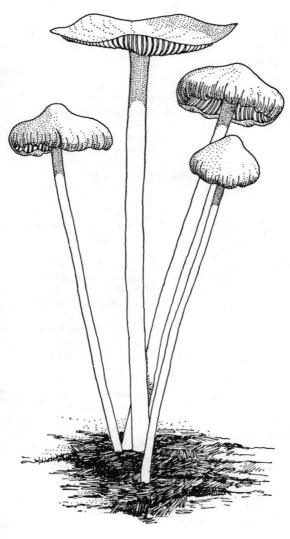

(23) Psilocybe strictipes
(natural size)

Psilocybe stuntzii Guzmán & Ott

Spore Print		dark purplish
Fruiting Cycle & Range		summer to fall, Oregon north to British Columbia, most common in Washington
Habit & Habitat		solitary to gregarious
Cap:	*Size*	1–4 cm.
	Shape	campanulate to convex expanding to plane as it ages
	Color	hygrophanous, dark brown drying to dark tan
	Surface	smooth, thin gelatinous pellicle, removable in wet weather, pellicle translucent
	Margin	smooth, incurved when young, radial lined
	Consistency	fragile
Stem:	*Size*	3–8 cm. long, 1–5 mm. wide
	Shape	straight and equal, sometimes bent and flattened
	Color	hygrophanous, brown drying dark tan
	Surface	smooth, covered with white powder, superior membranous annulus, darkened by falling spores
	Apex	not striate
	Base	not enlarged, covered with white mycelium
	Consistency	fragile
Gills:	*Color*	purple brown
	Attachment	adnate
	Edge	white when young
	Spacing	distant

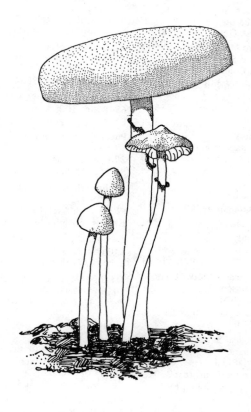

(24) **Psilocybe stuntzii**
(natural size)

Addresses for Information

British Mycological Society
33 Golf Course Rd.
Bonnyrig Midlothian
Scotland, U.K.

Cercle Des. Mycol.
1180 Rue Bleury
Montreal, Quebec, Canada

Colorado Mycological Society
909 York St.
Denver, Colorado 80206

Hoquiam Mushroom Club
Rt. 2, Box 193
Hoquiam, Washington 98550

Kitsap Peninsula Mushroom
Society
1132A Magnuson Way
Bremerton, Washington 98310

Lincoln County Mycological
Society
P.O. Box 94
Siletz, Oregon 97380

Los Angeles Mycological
Society
1615 N. Beverly Glen Blvd.
Los Angeles, California 90024

Mycological Society of San
Francisco
P.O. Box 904
San Francisco, California
94101

Mycological Society of Santa
Barbara
3194 Via Real
Carpenteria, California 93013

Mycological Society of
Toronto
14 Wicliffe Crescent
Willowdale, Ontario, Canada

New Jersey Mycological
Society
709 Reba Rd.
Landing, New Jersey 07850

New York Mycological Society
1700 York Ave.
New York, New York 10028

North American Mycological
Association
4245 Redinger Rd.
Portsmouth, Ohio 45662

North Idaho Mycological
Association
Rt. 5, Box 186
Post Falls, Idaho 83854

Oregon Mycological Society
6548 S.E. 30th Ave.
Portland, Oregon 97202

Puget Sound Mycological
Society
200 2nd Ave. N.
Seattle, Washington 98109

Snohomish Mycological
Society
12225 13th Ave. S.E.
Everett, Washington 99203

Tacoma Mushroom Society
1505 So. Mason
Tacoma, Washington 98405

Tri-Cities Mycological Society
1628 W. Clark
Pasco, Washington 99301

Analysis:

Drug Information Center
University of Oregon
1678 Columbia
Eugene, Oregon 97403

PharmChem Laboratories
1848 Bay Rd.
Palo Alto, California 94303

Glossary

Habit & Habitat

ANNUAL: completing growth in one year
CESPITOSE aggregated in tufts, but not grown together
CONIFER: cone bearing tree, evergreen
COPROPHILOUS: growing on dung
DEBRIS: the litter on the forest floor consisting of dead twigs, branches and leaves
GREGARIOUS: growing in groups, not in a clustered manner
HABIT: the manner of growth of a plant or fungus
HABITAT: natural place of growth
LIGNICOLOUS: growing on wood
MIXED WOODS: containing both broad-leaved trees and conifers
MYCORRHIZAL: a symbiotic relationship between fungi and tree roots
SCATTERED: fruiting bodies are grouped one or two feet apart
SOLITARY: growing singly
SUB-: as a prefix meaning less than, almost, somewhat or under
TERRESTRIAL: growing on the ground

Cap

APPENDICULATE: (of the margin) with fragments of veil
CAMPANULATE: bell-shaped
CONIC: taller than wide, cone shaped
CONVEX: regularly rounded with a greater width than height
DISC: center of the cap
ELEVATED: raised
GLOBOSE: spherical
HEMISPHERICAL: half sphere
HYGROPHANOUS: watery in appearance, with the moisture disappearing rapidly and the color fading
INCURVED: (of the margin) curved inwards towards the stem
IRREGULAR: not a constant shape
MARGIN: the outermost part of the cap

Cap Shapes

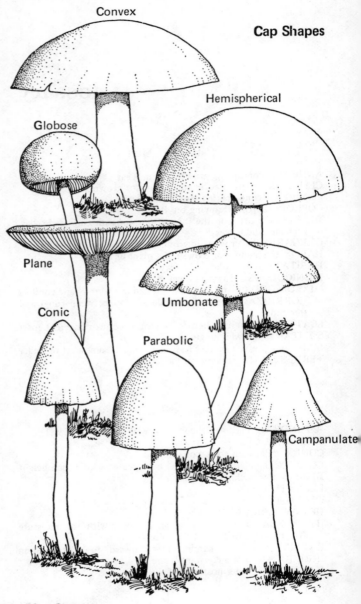

Convex

Hemispherical

Globose

Plane

Umbonate

Conic

Parabolic

Campanulate

MEMBRANOUS: thin and pliant like a membrane

OBTUSE: blunt or rounded

PALLID: of an indefinite pale appearance

PARABOLIC: regularly rounded with a greater height than width

PARTIAL VEIL: covering that extends from the (unopened) margin to the stem

PELLICLE: a skinlike layer on the cap, easily separated in wet weather

PILEUS; same as cap

PLANE: having a flat surface

PLIANT: flexible

RADIAL: like the spokes of a wheel

RETICULATE: net-like lines, veins or ridges which cross one another

STRIATE: having radiating lines or furrows

SUB-: as a prefix meaning less than, almost, somewhat or under

UMBO: a raised conical to convex knob or mound on the disc

UMBONATE: having an umbo

UNDULATING: (of the margin) wavy

VISCID: moist and sticky

WARTS: remnants of the universal veil

ZONE: concentric bands of color

Stem

ANNULUS: the ring or fibrils on the stem formed by the separation of the veil from the margin of the cap

APPRESSED: pressed against or lying against the surface or next to each other

BASE: bottom of the stem

CARTILAGINOUS: breaking with a snap, not pliant

CONCOLOROUS: of one color

CORTINA: marginal veil of spider web structure adhering to the stem *(Psilocybe)*

DILATED: (of the annulus) expanded, enlarged

EQUAL: uniform thickness

EVANESCENT: slightly developed and soon disappearing

FIBRILLOSE: covered with or composed of fibers

FIBRILS: minute fibers

MEMBRANOUS: thin and pliant like a membrane

OBLIQUE: (of the annulus) neither perpendicular nor horizontal, slanted

OVATE: (of the base) egg shaped

PALLID: of an indefinite pale appearance

PARTIAL VEIL: a membrane extending from the margin of the cap to the stem

PERSISTENT: (of the annulus) lasting, not disappearing

PITH: central stuffing in some stems

PLIANT: flexible

RUDIMENTARY: being or remaining in an imperfect state

STIPE: same as stem

STRIATE: having radial lines or furrows

UNIVERSAL VEIL: a substance surrounding the developing mushroom button *(Amanita)*

VISCID: moist and sticky

VOLVA: (of the base) remains of the universal veil, often in or beneath ground level *(Amanita)*

Gills

ADNATE: (attachment) entire width of gills attached to stem

ADNEXED: (attachment) narrowly attached to the stem

ASCENDING: extending upwards from the margin of the cap towards the apex of the stem

CLOSE: (spacing) when the gills are very close together, between crowded and distant

CROWDED: (spacing) when the gills are extremely close together

DECURRENT: (attachment) the gills run down the sides

DISTANT: (spacing) the gills are spaced far apart

FREE: (attachment) when the gills are not attached to the stem

GILL: knife-blade-like structure on the underside of the cap

LAMELLA: same as gill

MOTTLED: blotched with different colors

SPACING: a relative term describing the distance between the gills

SUB-: as a prefix meaning less than, almost, somewhat or under

UNCINATE: (attachment) hooklike

Scientific Reference Terms

BIOLOGY: the science of the life of plant and animal organisms

EXOTIC: foreign; not native

FAMILY: a group including all related genera, higher than a genus and designated by the ending "aceae"

FUNGI: plural of fungus

FUNGUS: nonflowering plant, devoid of chlorophyll, reproducing by spores and deriving sustenance from living or dead organic matter

Gill Spacing

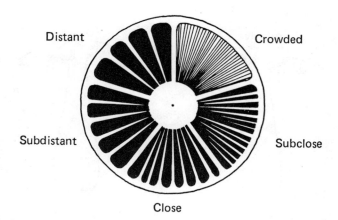

Distant

Crowded

Subdistant

Subclose

Close

GENERA: plural of genus

GENUS: a group of related species sharing certain similar characteristics

IDENTIFICATION: the study of the characteristics of an organism in order to determine to which species it belongs

MACROSCOPIC: visible without the aid of a microscope

MICROSCOPIC: visible only with the aid of a microscope

MYCOLOGIST: one who is versed in mycology

MYCOLOGY: the science of fungi

MYCOPHAGIST: one who eats mushrooms

MYCOPHOBE: one who abhors mushrooms

ORDER: a group of closely related families designated by the ending "-ales"

SPECIES: one or more individuals which show certain morphological and other characteristics, which are relatively constant throughout, and which are inherited or passed on from generation to generation

SUBGENUS: a group within a genus and containing groups of closely related species

TAXONOMY: the systematic classification of organisms, with emphasis on their natural relationships

VARIETY: a variation from the normal type of species

Gill Attachment

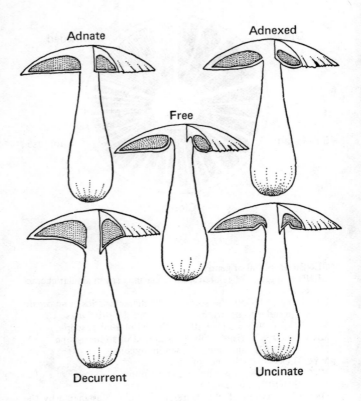

General

APEX: the tip of the part described

APPRESSED: pressed or lying flat against

BASIDIUM: (plural: BASIDIA) a microscopic structure on the gill surface which bears the spores

CENTIMETER: unit or metric measurement, the hundredth part of a meter—ten millimeters, or slightly less than half an inch

CONCENTRIC: having a common center

CONCOLOROUS: of one color

CONSISTENCY: the density, firmness or solidity of the part described

DOWNY: fine and soft

ECCENTRIC: off center

FAIRY RING: mushrooms growing naturally in a circle

FRUITING BODY: mushroom

HERBARIUM: a collection of dried plants or fungi arranged systematically

HUMUS: the mixture of decayed vegetation and soil in the forest

HYBRID: produced by interbreeding

HYPHA: (plural HYPHAE) one or more filamentous fungal cells

LATENT: potential for being present, but not a constant feature

MILLIMETER: unit of metric measurement—10 mm. equals 1 cm.

MYCELIUM: the mass of threads (hyphae) from which the mushroom grows

ORGANIC: living or dead animal or vegetable organisms

PARASITIC: growing on or in and getting sustenance from a living plant or animal

POISON: any substance which when introduced into an organism acts chemically to disrupt normal biological processes resulting in hazardous effects or death

PSYCHOACTIVE: capable of altering nervous system functioning

SPORES: reproductive bodies of fungi

SPORE PRINT: a mass of spores collected and used to determine their color

STERILE: producing no spores

SUB-: as a prefix meaning less than, almost, somewhat or under

SUPERFICIAL: easily removed

SYMBIOSIS: the coexistence in more or less mutual interdependence of two different organisms

TOADSTOOL: mushroom

TOXINS: any class of noxious or poisonous compounds

TRANSLUCENT: capable of transmitting light without being transparent

Glossary of Microscopic Characteristics

APEX: tip

APICAL: at the extreme end or top

APICULUS: point of attachment of spore to sterigma

BASIDIA: (singular BASIDIUM) cells that produce the spores

CAULOCYSTIDIA: sterile cells on the edge of the stem

CHEILOCYSTIDIA: sterile cells on the edge of the gill

COMPRESSED: flattened laterally

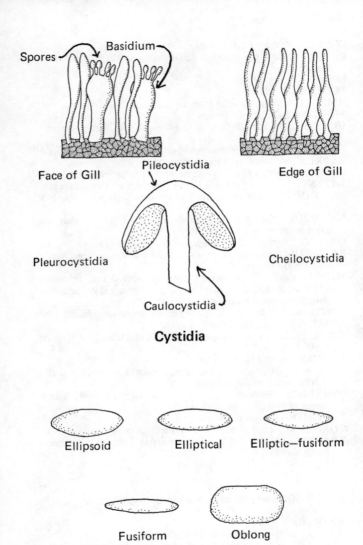

Spores — Basidium

Face of Gill

Pileocystidia

Edge of Gill

Pleurocystidia

Cheilocystidia

Caulocystidia

Cystidia

Ellipsoid   Elliptical   Elliptic—fusiform

Fusiform   Oblong

Spore Shapes

CYSTIDIA: sterile cells

ELLIPSOID: usually more than twice as long as broad, and curved in outline

ELLIPTICAL: the shape of an ellipse, rounded on the ends and sides and curved outward

ELLIPTICAL-FUSIFORM: more fusiform than elliptical

ELONGATE: to grow in length

FUSIFORM: spindle shaped

GUTTA: a tear

HYALINE: colorless

HYMENIUM the fertile spore-bearing layer of cells on the gills of the mushrooms

MICRON: (abbreviation μ) unit of metric measurement for use with a microscope—1000 μ equals 1 millimeter or 0.00004 of an inch

OBLONG: twice as long as wide with flattened ends

PORE: porous; small hole

PILEOCYSTIDIA: sterile cells on the cap

PLEUROCYSTIDIA: sterile cells on the face of the gill

STERIGMA; a tiny stalk on the basidium on which the spore is formed

TRUNCATE: an enlarged portion ending as if cut off

Microscopic Characteristics

1. *Amanita muscaria*
   9–11μ x 6–8μ smooth, ellipsoid, cheilocystidia present
2. *A. pantherina*
   10–15μ x 5–8μ smooth, elliptical, no pleurocystidia, cheilocystidia present
3. *Conocybe cyanopus*
   6.5–7.5μ x 4.5–5μ smooth, elliptical, unequal sided, small pore, caulocystidia and cheilocystidia present
4. *C. smithii*
   8–8.5μ x 4–4.5μ smooth, elongate ellipsoid with a small pore, caulocystidia and cheilocystidia present
5. *Gymnopilus spectabilis*
   8–10μ x 4.5–6μ rough, elliptical, pleurocystidia present
6. *Panaeolina foenisecii*
   12–17μ x 7–9μ warted, elliptical, pore at the apex, no pleurocystidia, cheilocystidia present
7. *Panaeolus acuminatus*
   13–16μ x 8–11μ smooth, elliptical with a large germ pore, no pleurocystidia, cheilocystidia present

8. *P. campanulatus*
   13–18μ x 8–13μ smooth, elliptical with a pore at the apex, no pleurocystidia, cheilocystidia present
9. *P. castaneifolius*
   12–18μ x 9–11μ warted, truncate, pore, pleurocystidia, pileocystidia and cheilocystidia present
10. *P. fimicola*
   11–12μ x 7–8μ smooth, subelliptical, few pleurocystidia, cheilocystidia present
11. *P. papilionaceus*
   14–15μ x 7–8μ smooth, elliptical with a central gutta, pleurocystidia, pileocystidia and cheilocystidia present
12. *P. phalaenarum*
   14–20μ x 8–11μ smooth, elliptical in face view, narrowly sub-elliptical in side view, apical pore hyaline, pleurocystidia and cheilocystidia present
13. *P. retirugis*
   11–14μ x 8–9μ smooth, elliptic-fusiform, no pleurocystidia, pileocystidia and cheilocystidia present
14. *P. semiovatus*
   15–20μ x 8–11μ smooth elliptic-fusiform with a pore at the apex, pileocystidia and cheilocystidia present
15. *P. sphinctrinus*
   13–14μ x 9–11.5μ smooth, elliptical with a hyaline germ pore, no pleurocystidia, cheilocystidia present
16. *P. subbalteatus*
   10–13μ x 6.5μ smooth, subelliptical in side view, apical hyaline pore, no pleurocystidia, cheilocystidia present
17. *Psilocybe baeocystis*
   11.5–13μ x 6.9–9μ smooth, oblong in face view, pleurocystidia and cheilocystidia present
18. *P. coprophila*
   11–15μ x 6.5–9μ smooth, elliptical with a pore at the apex, cheilocystidia present
19. *P. cubensis*
   13.3–14.9μ x 5.8–9μ smooth, nearly elliptical in side view, apex truncate, pleurocystidia and cheilocystidia present
20. *P. cyanescens*
   9–12μ x 6.9–9.2μ smooth, oblong in face view with broad germ pore, pleurocystidia and cheilocystidia present
21. *P. pelliculosa*
   9.3–12μ x 5–6μ smooth, ellipsoid (not compressed), pore, no pleurocystidia, cheilocystidia present
22. *P. semilanceata*
   10–15μ x 5–9.2μ smooth, ellipsoid (compressed), no pleurocystidia, cheilocystidia present

23. *P. strictipes*
    10–13μ x 6.9–9.2μ smooth, oblong in face view, unequal sided, apical germ pore, pleurocystidia and cheilocystidia present.
24. *P. stuntzii*
    10.1–12.5μ x 6–7.2μ smooth, ellipsoid, not truncate, germ pore small, no pleurocystidia, cheilocystidia present

Latin Glossary

Most scientific names in mycology and botany are derived from Latin or Greek. The scientific names applied to mushrooms and plants indicate one or more characteristics. Each mushroom or plant has two names: the first is the genus name and the second is the species name. The genus name *Psilocybe* means "naked head." The species name is sometimes used with a suffix, i.e. *Psilocybe stuntzii* or Stuntz's *Psilocybe.* This doesn't necessarily mean that he was the first to identify it, but that it was named for him. Often the names indicate the location where it was found, i.e. *Psilocybe cubensis,* the *Psilocybe* from Cuba. This doesn't mean that Cuba is the only place it grows, but that it was first found there. Taste, smell, color, shape and size are just a few of the characteristics designated by the names. A basic understanding of the Latin names will increase your understanding and make the task of identification easier.

AB: from or out of
ACUMINATUS: ending with a sharp point, i.e. *Panaeolus acuminatus*
AD: to, toward, against
AGRO: pertaining to fields or agriculture
ALBA, ALBO, ALBUM, ALBUS: white
AMERICANUS, –A, –UM: of the Americas
AMMOPHILUS: sand loving, i.e. *Psathyrella ammophila*
AMPLI: large
ANA: up
ANNUS, –A, –UM: annual, completing growth in one season
ANTE: before
ANTI: against
APRILIS: of the month of April
ARGENT: silvery
ARIDUS: dry
ARVENSIS: pertaining to a tilled field

ASTER, ASTRO: star shaped
AURI: ear shaped
AUTO: of the self
AUTUMNALIS: of the autumn, i.e. *Galerina autumnalis*
AZUREA: sky blue
BAEOCYSTIS: slim, short bladder, i.e. *Psilocybe baeocystis*
BI: two, twice
BISPORUS: with two spores on each basidium, i.e. *Agaricus bisporus [= A. brunnescens]*, the common mushroom bought in stores of America
BLANDIS, –A, –UM: mild
BREVI: short
BRUMALIS: of the winter solstice
BRYOPHILUS: moss loving
BULBI, BULBO: having a bulb
CAERULESCENS: caerulius sky blue, i.e. *Psilocybe caerulescens* (ESCENS: tending towards)
CAERULIPES: caerulius sky blue, i.e. *Psilocybe caerulipes* (PES: foot)
CALIFORNICUS, –A: of the state of California, i.e. *Psilocybe californica*
CAMPANULATE: bell shaped, i.e. *Panaeolus campanulatus*
CAMPESTRIS: pertaining to fields
CANADENSIS: of Canada
CANDID: pure white, i.e. *Psilocybe candidipes*
CAPNOIDES: smoky colored
CASTANEUS: the color of chestnuts, i.e. *Panaeolus castaneifolius*
CIBARIUS: edible
CLAVARIA: club, i.e. the genus *Clavaria* of the coral fungi
CLITOCYBE: slope head, i.e. the genus *Clitocybe*
CO: with
COMATUS, –A, –UM: covered with hair; shaggy
CONOCYBE: conical head, i.e. the genus *Conocybe*
CONTRA: against
COPROPHILA: growing on dung, i.e. *Psilocybe coprophila*
CORDYCEPS: club shaped head, i.e. the genus *Cordyceps*
CORONILLA: small crown, i.e. *Stropharia coronilla*
CORTINA: cobweblike veil, curtain
CRISPA: closely curled
CUBENSIS: of cuba, i.e. *Psilocybe cubensis*
CUSPI: sharp point
CYANESCENS: becoming deep blue, i.e. *Psilocybe cyanescens*
DE: from
DEALBATUS: bleached, white
DECORA, –UM: decorative
DECURRENS: running down

DELICIOSUS: delicious

DENTI, DENS: toothed, i.e. the genus *Dentinum* of the tooth fungi

DERMI, DERMIS: skin

DI, DIS: two, double

ECO: habitat

EDULIS: edible, i.e. *Boletus edulis* or the plant *Catha edulis*

EMETICA: induces vomiting, i.e. *Russula emetica*

ENTOLOMA: with the margin inwards, fringed, i.e. the genus *Entoloma*

ERECTA, –UM: erect or upright

ESCULENTUS, –A, –UM: edible

EU: true

EX, E: from, out of, down, without

FASCI: clustered or grouped

FIBROSIS: fibrous

FIMICOLA: fimus: dung, cola: to inhabit, i.e. *Panaeolus fimicola*

FISTULOSUS: hollow like a tube, i.e. the genus *Fistulina* of the polypores

FOENISECII: haymaker, i.e. *Panaeolina foenisecii*

FOETENS: ill-smelling, nauseating

FOMENTARIUS: a substance that can be used as tinder to light a fire, i.e. *Fomes fomentarius*

FOMES: a substance that catches fire easily, i.e. the genus *Fomes* of the polypores

FORMOSUS, –A: beautiful

FRAGILIS, –E: fragile

FRAGRANS: fragrant

FUMI: smoky gray

FUSCUS: dark

GALERA: like a cap

GALERINA: diminutive of *Galera,* i.e. the genus *Galerina*

GEASTER: star of the earth, i.e. the genus *Geastrum* is closely related to the puffballs

GELATINOSUS: gelatinous, like jelly

GLABROUS: hairless; smooth

GLUTINOSUS, –A, –UM: sticky

GOMPHIDIUS: similar to a nail, i.e. the genus *Gomphidius*

GOMPHUS: club, i.e. the genus *Gomphus*

GYMNOPILUS: naked cap, i.e. the genus *Gymnopilus*

GYNO, GYNUS: female

GYRO: circular

HAEMO: blood red

HAPLO: one

HEMI: half; partial

HEMISPHAERICUS: half sphere

HERICUM: pertaining to the hedgehog, i.e. the genus *Hericium*
HETERO: various; diverse
HIEMALIS: of winter
HOMO: the same
HORTI: of gardens
HYALINE: transparent; clear
HYDRA, −O: water
HYGROPHORUS: bearer of moisture, i.e. the genus *Hygrophorus*
HYPER: above
HYPHA, −AE: web
HYPHOLOMA: with a fringed margin
IDAHOENSIS, −E: of Idaho
ILLUSTRI: brilliant
INOCYBE: fibrous head, i.e. the genus *Inocybe*
INTER: between, among
INTERMEDIUS: intermediate, i.e. *Psathyrella intermedius*
INTRA, INTRO: within; inside
ISO: equal
JAPONICUS, −A, −UM: of Japan
KINETO: movement
LABIA: lip
LATI: wide
LEVIS: smooth
LOMA: edge or border, fringe
LONGI: long
LUBRICUS: slippery; smooth
LUCIOUS, −A, −UM: glossy, polished; shiny
LUNA: moon
MACRO: long or large
MAJOR: larger or bigger
MAPPA: napkin, i.e. *Amanita mappa*
MARGINATA: distinctly marked border, i.e. *Galerina marginata*
MARZULOUS: of the month of March
MAXIMUS, −A, −UM: largest
MEAS, MEASO: medium
MEDIO: middle
MEGA: large
MEIO: less
MELANO: black
META: with, sharing or beyond
MEXICANA: of Mexico, i.e. *Psilocybe mexicana*
MIA, MAJA, MAILIS: of the month of May
MICRO: small
MINIMUS, −A, −UM: smallest
MINOR, MINUS: smaller
MIRABILIS: wonderful, i.e. *Boletus mirabilis*
MONO: one

MONTI, MONTANUS: growing in the mountains, i.e. *Psilocybe montana*

MUSCA, MUSCARIUS: of flies, i.e. *Amanita muscaria*

MYC, MYCET, MYCETO: of fungus

NAEMATOLOMA: with filament along margin, i.e. the genus *Naematoloma*

NANUS, −A, −UM: dwarf

NECRO, NECATOR: dead or killer

NIDU: nest, i.e. the genus *Nidularia* of the bird's nest fungi

NIMBATUS: cloudy

NOLANEA: like a bell

NON: not

NOTHO: false

NOVI, NOVA: new

NUBI; cloudy

NUDI, NUDUS: naked

NYCTA: night

OB: reversed, against

OCCIDENTALIS: western

ODORA: fragrant

OFFICINALIS, −E: used as a drug or medicine, i.e. *Polyporus officinalis*

OMNI: all

OMPHAL: bellybutton

OPTIMUS, −A, −UM: best

ORBICULA: round or flat

OREGONENSIS: from Oregon or the Oregon Territory

OSTREATUS: of oysters, i.e. the Oyster Mushroom, *Pleurotus ostreatus*

OVALI, −A, −I, −US: oval or egg shaped

PALLIDES, −A, −UM: pale

PALUDI, PALUSTRIS: of swampy places

PANAEOLUS: dazzling, all-variegated, i.e. the genus *Panaeolus*

PANTHERINUS: pertaining to the panther, i.e. *Amanita pantherina*

PAPILIO: a butterfly, i.e. *Panaeolus papilionaceus*

PARA: beside or near

PARVI: small

PELLICULOSA: provided with a pellicle, i.e. *Psilocybe pelliculosa*

PENDULUS, −A, −UM: hanging, pendant

PERENNIS, −E: perennial; continuing growth from year to year

PHALLOIDES: similar to phallus, i.e. *Amanita phalloides*

PHALLUS: swollen or puffed up, penis

PHILO, −E: lover of, or friend

PHOTO: light

PHYT, −O, −UM: a plant

PILEUS, −A: a cap
PINI: of pine trees
PIPERATUS: peppery
PLACOMYCES: flat mushrooms
PLURI: several
PLEUROTUS: with the ear on one side, i.e. the genus *Pleurotus*
PLUTEUS: bracket or console, i.e. the genus *Pluteus*
PODUS, −U, −UM: foot
POLI: white or gray; polished
POLY: many
POLYPORUS: many pores, i.e. the genus *Polyporus*
POST: after
PRIMA, −US: first
PRUINOSUS: finely powdered
PSATHYRA: fragile
PSATHYRELLA: diminutive of psathyra, i.e. the genus *Psathyrella*
PSEUDO: false
PSILOCYBE: naked head, i.e. the genus *Psilocybe*
PUBESCENS: becoming downy
PYRO: fire
QUAD: four
RADICA, RADICANS: taking root; rooted
RAMARIA: pertaining to branches, i.e. the genus *Ramaria* of the coral fungi
RE: backwards
RECTUS, −A, −UM: straight; upright
RETICULATUS: woven, net-like
RETIRUGIS: a net or wrinkle, i.e. *Panaeolus retirugis*
RETRO: backwards
RHIZOPOGON: bearded root, i.e. the genus *Rhizopogon*
ROTUNDE, −US, −A, −UM: round
SACC, −I, −O, −US: a sack
SAPIDUS, −A, −UM: good taste
SAPRO: rotten
SARDONIUS: very bitter
SATANAS: pertaining to satan
SATIVUS, −A, −UM: planted; cultivated, i.e. *Cannabis sativa*
SCLERO: hard, i.e. the genus *Scleroderma*
SEMI: half; partial
SEMILANCEATA: shaped like a half lance, i.e. *Psilocybe semilanceata*
SEMIOVATUS: shaped like a half egg, i.e. *Panaeolus semiovatus*
SEPULCHRALIS: growing in burial places, i.e. *Psathyrella sepulchralis*
SEROTINE: late
SILVATICUS: wild of the woods, i.e. *Psilocybe silvatica*

SIMPLEX: in one piece
SOL, −A: sun, sunlight
SOLIDIPES: solid foot, i.e. *Panaeolus solidipes*
SOLITARIUS: solitary
SPECTABILIS: admirable; wonderful, i.e. *Gymnopilus spectabilis*
SPHINCTRINUS: like tightening with a string, i.e. *Panaeolus sphinctrinus*
SQUAMO: scaly
SQUARROSUS: rough
STRICTIPES: thin foot, i.e. *Psilocybe strictipes*
STRICTUS, −A, −UM: narrow and straight
SUB: almost
SUBBALTEATUS: with a not too conspicuous belt, i.e. *Panaeolus subbalteatus*
SUPER: above
TELE: afar
TENAX: strong
TERMINALIS, −E: ending
TERRESTRIS, −E: of land
THERMO: heat
TINCTORIUS, −A, −UM: used for dyeing
TRANS: across
TREMELLOSUS: quivering, i.e. the genus *Tremella* of the jelly fungi
TRI, TRIPLO: three
TRICHOLOMA: with hair along the margin, i.e. the genus *Tricholoma*
TROPO: movement towards
TURGID: full
ULTRA: beyond
UMBEL: umbrella shaped
UMBONATUS, −A, −UM: with a convex elevation (umbo) in the center
UNDULATUS, −A, −UM: wavy
UNI: one
USITI, USITUS: useful
VARIEGATUS, −A, −UM: irregularly colored
VARIUS, −A, −UM: differing; diverse
VENA: veined
VENENO, VENENA: poisonous, i.e. *Galerina venenata*
VERNIS, −A, −UM: of spring
VERSI: changing
VERSICOLOR: multicolored
VIROSUS: poisonous, i.e. *Amanita virosa*
VISCIDI, −US: sticky; viscid
VOLVA: covering or sac
VULGARIUS, −E: common, known

WASHINGTONENSIS: of Washington, i.e. *Psilocybe washingtonensis*

XENO: stranger

XERO: dry

XYLO, –UM: wood

ZONATUS, ZONA: banded, zoned

Common Suffixes

ACEAE: belonging to the family of

ALIS: belonging to

AGEUS, –A, –UM: like

ASCENS: becoming something

CEPS: head

COLUS, –A, –UM: dwelling; living on

ELLIS, –ARIS, –ATUS: diminutive; smaller

ENSIS, –E: of or pertaining to; from; i.e. *Psilocybe cubensis*

ERRIMUS, –A: very

ESCENS: tending towards, i.e. *Psilocybe cyanescens*

FERUS, –A, –UM: bearing; carrying

FORMIS, –E: form; shape

IDES, IDEUS: similarity

INUS: a resemblance

ISSIMUS, –A, –UM: very

ODES, OIDES: similar to, i.e. *Amanita phalloides*

OPSIS: likeness; similarity

OSA, –US, –UM: largeness

PEDA, PEDIS, PES, PODA, PUS: foot, i.e. *Psilocybe strictipes*

PHORUS, –A, –UM: bearing

Bibliography

Agurell, S., Blomkvist, S., & Catalfomo, P., 1966. Biosynthesis of psilocybin in submerged culture of *Psilocybe cubensis*. *Acta Pharm. Suecia* 3:37–44.

————, & Nilsson, L., 1968. Biosynthesis of psilocybin: Part II. *Acta Chemica Scandinavica* 4:1210–1218.

————, & ————, 1968. A biosynthesis sequence from tryptophan to psilocybin. *Tetrahedron Letters* 9:1063–1064.

Allegro, J., 1970. *The Sacred Mushroom and the Cross*. Doubleday, New York.

Ames, R., 1958. The influence of temperature on mycelial growth of *Psilocybe, Panaeolus,* and *Copelandia*. *Mycopath. et Mycol. Appl.* 9:268–274

Armstrong, C.D., 1952. Two deaths in California by *Amanita phalloides*. *Standford Med. Bull.* 13:111–116.

Barron, F., & Jarvik, M.E., 1964. The Hallucinogenic Drugs. *Sci. Amer.* 210: No. 4.

Benedict, R.G., Brady, L.R., Smith, A.H., & Tyler, V.E. Jr., 1962. Occurence [sic] of psilocybin and psilocin in certain *Conocybe* and *Psilocybe* Species. *Lloydia* 25:156–159.

————, ————, & Tyler, V.E. Jr., 1962. Occurrence of psilocin in *Psilocybe baeocystis*. *J. Pharm. Sci.* 51:393–394.

————, ————, Spurr, J., & Stuntz, D.E., 1970. Occurrence of the deadly *Amanita verna* in the Pacific Northwest. *Mycologia* 62:597–599.

————, & Tyler, V.E. Jr., 1962. Examination of mycelial cultures of *Panaeolus* species for tryptophan hydroxylase activity. *Lloydia* 25:46–54.

————, ————, & Brady, L.R., 1966. Chemotaxonomic significance of isoxazole derivatives in *Amanita* species. *Lloydia* 29:333.

————, ————, & Watling, R., 1967. Blueing in *Conocybe, Psilocybe* and a *Stropharia* Species and the detection of Psilocybin. *Lloydia* 30:150–157.

Bodin, F., & Cheinisse, C.F., 1970. *Poisons*. McGraw-Hill, New York.

Brady, L.R., & Tyler, V.E. Jr., 1959. A chromatographic examination of the alkaloidal fraction of *Amanita pantherina*. *J. Amer. Pharm. Assoc.* 48:417–419.

_____, Benedict, R.G., & Tyler, V.E. Jr., 1975. Identification of *Conocybe filaris* as a toxic basidiomycete. *Lloydia* 38:172–173.

Brown, J.K., & Malone, M.H., 1973. Status of drug quality in the street drug market. *Pacific Information on Street Drugs* 1:1–7.

Buck, R.W., 1961. Mushroom poisoning since 1924 in the United States. *Mycologia* 53:537–538.

_____, 1967. Psychedelic effect of *Pholiota spectabilis*. *New England J. Med.* 267:391–392.

Castaneda, C., 1968. *The Teachings Of Don Juan*. Ballantine, New York.

Catalfomo, P., & Tyler, V.E. Jr., 1964. The production of psilocybin in submerged culture by *Psilocybe cubensis*. *Lloydia* 27:53–63.

_____, & Eugster, C., 1970. *Amanita muscaria:* present understanding of its chemistry. *Bull. Narc.* 22:23–41.

Cheymel, J., 1966. Hallucinogens incapacitants. *Information Médicale et Paramédicale* 18: No. 5. Montreal.

Chilton, W.S., & Ott, J., 1976. Toxic Metabolites of *Amanita pantherina*, *A. cothurnata*, *A. muscaria* and other *Amanita* species. *Lloydia* 39:150–157.

Clarke, J.M., & Peck, C.H., 1909. Report of the State Botanist, 1908. Bull. N.Y. State Museum. 131:37.

Dearness, J., 1911. The personal factor in mushroom poisoning. *Mycologia* 3:75–78.

Delay, J., Pichet, P., Lemperiere, T., Nicolas-Charles, P., 1958. Effets Psycho-physiologiques de la psilocybine. *Comp. Rend. Acad. Sci.,* Paris 247:1235.

_____, _____, _____, _____, & Quetin, A., Part I: Les effets somatiques de la psilocybine. 1959. Part II: Les effets psychiques de la psilocybine et perspectives thérapeutiques. *Ann. Méd. Psychol.* 117:891–899, 899–907.

Dennis, LaRae, 1972. *Name Your Poison: A Guide to Cultivated and Native Oregon Plants Toxic to Humans*. Oregon State University.

Dennis, R., & Wakefield, R., 1946. New and interesting British fungi. *Trans. Brit. Mycol. Soc.* 29:141.

———, 1961. Fungi venezuelani, IV. *Kew Bull.* 15:57–156.

Douglas, B., 1917. Mushroom poisoning. *Torreya* 17:171–175, 207–221.

Duke, R., & Keeler, M., 1968. The effects of psilocybin, dextroamphetamine and placebo on performance of the trail making test. *J. Clin. Psychol.* 24:316–317.

Earle, F.S., 1906. Algunos (hongos) Cubanos. *Inf. An. Estae. Agron Cuba* 1:225–242.

Enos, L., 1970. *A Key to the American Psilocybin Mushroom.* Youniverse, Lemon Grove, Cal.

Fisher, R., & Warshaw, D., 1969. Psilocybin-induced autonomic, perceptual, and behavioral change. *Pharmakopsychiatrie* 1:291–302.

———, Hill, R.M., & Warshaw, D., 1969. Effects of the Psychodysleptic drug psilocybin on visual perception. *Experientia* 25:166–169.

Ford, W., 1907. A clinical study of mushroom intoxication. *Johns Hopkins Hospital Bull.* 18:123–130.

Furst, P.T., 1976. *Hallucinogens and Culture.* Chandler & Sharp, San Francisco, Cal.

Gessner, P.K., Khairallah, P.A., McIsaac, W.M., & Page, I.H., 1960. The relationship between the metabolic rate and pharmacological actions of serotonin, bufotenine and psilocybin. *J. Pharmacol.* 130:126–133.

Glen, G., 1816. A case proving the deleterious effects of the *Agaricus campanulatus,* which was mistaken for the *Agaricus campestris. London Med. Physiol. J.* 36:451–453.

Graves, R., 1962. A journey to paradise. *Holiday* 32:36.

Guzmán, G., 1959. Sinopsis de los conocimientos sobre los hongos alucinógenes mexicanos. *Bol. Soc. Bot. Mex.* 24:14–34.

———, 1972. Las especies conocidas del género *Panaeolus* en México. *Bol. Soc. Bot. Mex.* 24:14–34.

———, 1976. Description and chemical analysis of a new species of hallucinogenic *Psilocybe* from the Pacific Northwest. *Mycologia* 68:1261–1267.

———, Ott, J., Boydston, J., & Pollock, S.H., 1976. Psychotropic mycoclora of Washington, Idaho, Oregon, California and British Columbia. *Mycologia* 68:1267–1272.

Haard, R., & K., 1976. *Poisonous & Hallucinogenic Mushrooms.* Cloudburst Press, Seattle, Washington.

Harkness, & Moore, 1876. Catalog of the Pacific Coast fungi. *Cal. Acad. Sci.*

Harner, M.J., editor, 1973. *Hallucinogens and Shamanism.* Oxford University, London.

Harris, B., 1976. *Growing Wild Mushrooms.* Wingbow Press, Berkeley, Cal.

Hatfield, G.M., & Brady, L.R., 1969. Occurrence of bis-noryangonin in *Gymnopilus spectabilis. J. Pharm. Sci.* 58:1298–1299.

_____, 1971. Occurrence of bis-noryangonin and hispidin in *Gymnopilus* species. *Lloydia* 34:260–263.

_____, & Brady, L.R., 1975. Toxins of higher fungi. *Lloydia* 38:36–55

Heim, R., 1957. Analyse de quelques expériences personelles produites par l'ingestion des Agarics hallucinogenes du Mexique. *Comp. Rend. Acad. Sci.* 245:597–603.

_____, 1957. Hallucinatory mushrooms used by the Indians of Central and South America. *Proc. Ninth Pac. Sci. Congr.* p. 75.

_____, Hofmann, A., Brack, A., Kobel, H., 1958. Psilocybin ein psychotroper Wirkstoff aus dem mexikankischen Rauschpilz. *Experientia* 14:107–109.

_____, _____, 1958. Isolement de la psilocybine à partir du *Stropharia cubensis* Earle et d'autres espèces de champignons hallucinogènes mexicains appartenant au genre *Psilocybe. Comp. Rend. Acad. Sci.* 247:557–561.

_____, & Wasson, R.G., 1958. *Les Champignons Hallucinogènes du Mexique.* Archives du Mus. Nat. d'Hist. Nat., Paris, Series 7, Vol. 6.

_____, 1963. *Les Champignons toxiques et hallucinogènes.* N. Boubee, Paris.

_____, 1965. Les substances indoliques produites par les champignons toxiques et hallucinogènes. *Bull. de Med. Leg.* 8:122–141.

_____, & Wasson, R.G., 1965. The mushroom madness of Kuma. *Bot. Mus. Leaf. Harvard Univ.* 21:1–36.

_____, 1966. Histoire de la Découverte des champignons hallucinogènes du Mexique. *Collogue Intern. C. N. R. S.* 144:243–264.

—————, Genest, K., Hughes, D.W., Bolec, G., 1966. Botanical and chemical characterization of a forensic mushroom specimen of the genus *Psilocybe*. *J. Forensic Sci. Soc.* 6:192–201.

—————, 1971. A propos des propriétés hallucinogènes du *Psilocybe semilanceata*. *Le Naturaliste Canadien* 98:415–424.

Hoffer, A., & Osmond, H., 1967. *The Hallucinogens*. Academic Press, New York.

Hofmann, A., Frey, A., Ott, H., Petrzilka, T., & Troxler, F., 1958. Konstitutionsaufklärung und Synthese von Psilocybin. *Experientia* 14:397–401.

—————, Heim, R., Brack, A., Kobel, H., Frey, A., Ott, H., Petrzilka, T., & Toxler, F., 1959. Psilocybin und Psilocin, zwei psychotrope Wirkstoffe aus mexikanischen Rauschpilzen. *Hel. Chim. Acta.* 42:1557–1572.

—————, & Troxler, F., 1959. Identifizierung von Psilocin. *Experientia* 15:101–104.

—————, 1959. Psychotomimetic drugs: Chemical and pharmacological aspect. *Acta Physiol. Pharmacol. Neerl.* 8:240–258.

—————, Heim, R., & Tscherter, H., 1963. Présence de la psilocybine dans une espéce europèenne d'agaric, le *Psilocybe semilanceata. Comp. Rend. Acad. Sci.* 257:10–12.

Hollister, L.E., 1961. Clinical, biochemical and psychologic effects of psilocybin. *Arch. Int. Pharm.* 130:42–52.

—————, 1968. *Chemical Psychoses: LSD and Related Compounds.* C.C. Thomas, Springfield, Ill.

Horita, A., 1963. Some biochemical studies on psilocybin and psilocin. *J. Neuropsychiatry* 4:270–273.

—————, & Weber, L.J., 1961. Dephosphorylation of psilocybin to psilocin by alkaline phosphatase. *Proc. Soc. Exper. Biol. Med.* 106:32–34.

Hotson, J.W., 1934. One death in Anacortes, Washington by *Amanita pantherina. Mycologia* 26:194.

Huxley, A., 1954. *The Doors of Perception and Heaven and Hell.* Harper & Row, New York.

—————, 1962. *Island.* Harper & Brothers, New York.

Isbell, H., 1959. Comparison of the relations induced by psilocybin and LSD-25 in man. *Psychopharmacologia* 1:29.

—————, Miner, E.J., Wikler, A., & Wolback, A.B., 1961. Cross tolerance between LSD and psilocybin. *Psychopharmacologia* 2:147–159.

Janiger, O., 1959. The use of hallucinogenic agents in psychiatry. *Calif. Clin.* 55:222–224, 251–259.

Johnson, D.W., & Gunn, J.W., 1972. Dangerous drugs; adulterants, dilutents and deception in street samples. *J. Forensic Sci.* 4:629–639.

Keeler, M.H., 1965. Similarity of schizophrenia and the psilocybin syndrome as determined by objective methods. *Intern. J. Neuropsych.* 1:630–634.

_____, 1965. The effects of psilocybin on a test of afterimage perception. *Psychopharmacol.* 8:131–139.

Kühner, R., & Romagnesi, H., 1953. *Flore analyique des champignons supérieurs.* Masson, Paris.

Lampe, K.F., 1973. Mushroom poisoning in the young child, *Paediatrician* 2.83.

Largent, D., 1973. *How To Identify Mushrooms (To Genus) Using Only Macroscopic Features.* Mad River Press, Eureka, Cal.

Leary, T., Litwin, G.H., & Metzner, R., 1963. Reactions to psilocybin administered in a supportive environment. *J. Nervous Mental Disease* 137:561–573.

Leung, A.Y., Smith, A.H., & Paul, A.G., 1965. Production of psilocybin in *Psilocybe baeocystis,* saprophytic culture. *J. Pharm. Sci.* 54:1576–1579.

_____, & Paul, A.G., 1967. Baeocystin, a monomethyl analog of psilocybin in *Psilocybe baeocystis,* saprophytic culture. *J. Pharm. Sci.* 56:146.

_____, _____, 1968. Baeocystin and norbaeocystin; new analogs of psilocybin from *Psilocybe baeocystis. J. Pharm. Sci.* 57:1667–1671.

_____, _____, 1969. The relationship of carbon and nitrogen nutrition of *Psilocybe baeocystis* to the production of psilocybin and its analogs. *Lloydia* 32:66–71.

Levine, M., 1919. The sporadic appearance of non-edible mushrooms in cultures of *Agaricus campestris. Bull. Torrey Botan. Club* 46:57–63.

Lilly, J., 1972. *The Center Of The Cyclone.* Julian Press, New York.

McCawley, E.L., Brumnett, R.E., & Dana, G.W., 1962. Convulsions from *Psilocybe* mushroom poisoning. *Western Pharmacol. Soc.* 5:27–33.

Metzner, R., Litwin, G., & Weil, G.M., 1965. The relation of expectation and mood to psilocybin reactions. *Psychedel. Rev.* 5:3–39.

Michaux, H., 1960. La psilocybine. *Rev. Mycol.* 1:25.

Miller, O.K. Jr., 1968. Fungi of the Yukon and Alaska. *Mycologia* 60:1201–1203.

————, 1972. *Mushrooms of North America*. E.P. Dutton & Co., New York.

Murrill, W.A., 1909. A new poisonous mushroom. *Mycologia* 1:211–214.

————, 1910. Poisonous mushrooms. *Mycologia* 2:255–264.

————, 1916. A very dangerous mushroom, *Panaeolus venenosus,* sp. nov. *Mycologia* 8:186–187.

————, 1923. Dark spored agarics, V, *Psilocybe, Mycologia* 15:1–22.

Ola'h, G.M., 1968. Etude chimotaxinomique sur les *Panaeolus. Comp. Rend. Acad. Sci.* 267:1369–1372.

————, 1969. A taxonomical *[sic]* and physiological study of the genus *Panaeolus* with Latin descriptions of the new species. *Rev. Mycol.* 33:284–290.

————, 1969. *Le Genre Panaeolus: Essai taxonomique et physiologique.* Memoire Hors-Serie 10, *Rev. Mycol.,* Paris.

Orr, R.T., & D.B., 1968. *Mushrooms of Southern California.* U. of Cal., Berkeley, Cal.

Oss, O.T., & Oeric, O.N., 1976. *Psilocybin: Magic Mushroom Grower's Guide.* And/Or Press, Berkeley, Cal.

Ott, J., & Guzmán, G., 1976. Detection of psilocybin in species of *Psilocybe, Panaeolus,* and *Psathyrella. Lloydia* 39:258–260.

————, 1976. *Hallucinogenic Plants of North America.* Wingbow Press, Berkeley, Cal.

————, 1976. Psycho-mycological studies of *Amanita* from ancient sacrament to modern phobia. *J. Psychedel. Drugs* 8:27–35.

Pollock, S.H., 1974. A novel experience with *Panaeolus:* a case study from Hawaii. *J. Psychedel. Drugs* 6:85–89.

————, 1975. Psilocybin mushroom pandemic. *J. Psychedel. Drugs* 7:73–84.

————, 1976. Psilocybian mycetismus with special reference to *Panaeolus. J. Psychedel. Drugs* 8:43–57.

Puget Sound Mycological Society, 1972. *Mushroom Poisoning in the Pacific Northwest.*

Puharich, A., 1974. *The Sacred Mushroom.* Doubleday, New York.

Repke, D.B., & Leslie, D.T., 1977. Baeocystin in *Psilocybe semilanceata. J. Pharm Sci.,* 66:113–114.

——————, ——————, Mandell, D.M., & Kish, N., 1977. Gas chromatographic-mass spectral analysis of psilocin and psilocybin. (in press) *J. Pharm. Sci.*

Rinaldi, A., & Tyndale, V., 1972. *The Complete Book of Mushrooms.* Crown, New York.

Robbers, J.E., Tyler, V.E. Jr., & Ola'h, G.M., 1969. Additional evidence supporting the occurrence of psilocybin in *Panaeolus foenisecii. Lloydia* 32:399–400.

Robinson, R.K., 1967. *Ecology of Fungi.* English University Press, London.

Rolfe, R.T., & F.W., 1925. *The Romance of the Fungus World.* Reprint 1974. Dover, New York.

Romagnesi, H., 1947. Description des especes *Panaeolus retirugis. Bull. Soc. Linn. Lyon.* 16:77–78.

Ruzickova, R., Bily, D., Konias, V., & Soucek, Z., 1966. The effects of psilocybin in chronic schizophrenia. *Activitas Nervosa Superior* 8:222–223.

——————, ——————, Vyhnankova, M., Dubanksy, B., Konias, V., & Soucek, Z., 1966. Clinical effects of psilocybin in chronic schizophrenics. *Activitas Nervosa Superior* 8:346–347.

Rynearson, R.R., Wilson, M.R., & Bickford, R.G., 1968. Psilocybin-induced changes in psychologic function, electroencephalogram, and light-evoked potentials in human subjects. *Mayo Clinic Proc.* 43:191–204.

Sanford, J., 1973. *In Search of the Magic Mushroom.* Potter, New York.

Sanford, J.H., 1971. Japan's laughing mushrooms. *Economic Botany* 26:174–181.

Schultes, R.E., & Hofmann, A., 1973. *The Botany and Chemistry of Hallucinogens.* C.C. Thomas. Springfield, Ill.

——————, 1976. *Hallucinogenic Plants.* Golden Press, New York.

Simons, D.M., 1971. The mushroom toxins. *Delaware Med. J.* 43:177.

Singer, R., & Smith, A.H., 1958. New species of *Psilocybe. Mycologia* 50:141–142.

————————, ————————, 1958. Mycological investigation on Teonánacatl, the Mexican mushroom: Part I, the history of Teonánacatl, field work and culture work. Part II, a taxonomic monograph of *Psilocybe,* section Caerulescentes. *Mycologia* 50:239–303.

————————, 1975. *The Agaricales in Modern Taxonomy.* Third Edition, J. Cramer, Vaduz.

Smith, A.H., 1937. New or unusual agarics from the Western United States. *Mycologia* 29:45–59.

————————, 1941. Studies on North American agarics. *Cent. Univ. Mich. Herb.* 5:1–73.

————————, 1948. Studies on dark-spored agarics. *Mycologia* 40:699–707.

————————, 1949. *Mushrooms in their Natural Habitats.* Sawyer's Inc., Portland, Oregon.

————————, & Singer, R., 1964. *A Monograph on the Genus Galerina Earle.* Hafner, Darien, Conn.

————————, 1975. *A Field Guide to Western Mushrooms.* Univ. Mich. Ann Arbor, Mich.

Snell, W., & Dick, E.A., 1971. *A Glossary of Mycology.* (revised edition) Harvard, Cambridge, Mass.

Stein, S.I., 1958. Observations on agarics causing cerebral mycetisms. Part I, An unusual effect from species of Mexican mushroom *Psilocybe cubensis. Mycopathol.* 9:263–267.

————————, Closs, G.L., & Gabel, N.W., 1959. Observations on psycho neurophysiologically significant mushrooms. *Mycopathol.* 11:205–216.

————————, 1959. Clinical observations on the effects of *Panaeolus venenosus* versus *Psilocybe caerulescens* mushrooms. *Mycologia* 51:49–50.

Stolman, A., 1963. *Progress in Chemical Toxicology.* Academic Press, New York.

Tyler, V.E. Jr., 1958. Occurrence of serotonin in a hallucinogenic mushroom. *Science* 128:718.

————————, & Malone, M.H., 1960. An investigation of the culture, constituents, and physiological activity of *Panaeolus campanulatus. J. Amer. Pharm. Assoc.* 49:23–27.

————————, 1961. Indole derivatives in certain North American mushrooms. *Lloydia* 24:71–74.

————————, 1963. Poisonous mushrooms. *Prog. Chem. Toxicol.* 1:339.

_____, & Smith, A.H., 1963. Chromatographic detection of Amanita toxins in *Galerina venenata. Mycologia* 55:358.

_____, Benedict, R.G., Brady, L.R., Khanna, J.M., & Malone, M.H., 1963. Chromatographic and pharmacologic evaluation of some toxic *Galerina* species. *Lloydia* 26:154–157.

_____, & Grogor, D., 1964. Occurrence of 5-hydroxytryptamine and 5-hydroxytryptophan in *Panaeolus sphinctrinus. J. Pharm. Sci.* 53:590–593.

_____, Benedict, R.G., Brady, L.R., & Robbers, F.E., 1966. Occurrence of amanita toxins in American collections of deadly *Amanitas. J. Pharm. Sci.* 55:590–593.

Velle, E., & Maefie, W., 1964. Mushroom poisoning. *J. Royal Army Med. Corps* 110.

Walters, M.B., 1965. *Pholiota spectabilis,* a hallucinogenic fungus. *Mycologia* 57:837–838.

Wasson, R.G., 1957. Seeking the Magic mushroom. *Life* 3:100–120.

Wasson, V.P., & R.G., 1957. *Mushrooms, Russia and History.* Pantheon Books, New York.

_____, _____, 1958. The hallucinogenic mushrooms. *Garden J. N.Y. Bot. Gardens, N.Y.*

Wasson, R.G., 1958. The divine mushrooms; primitive religion and hallucinatory agents. *Proc. Amer. Phil. Soc.* 102:221–223.

_____, & Heim, R., 1959. The hallucinogenic mushrooms of Mexico: an adventure in ethnomycological exploration. *Trans. N.Y. Acad. Sci.* 21:325–339.

_____, 1972. *Soma, Divine Mushroom of Immortality.* Harcourt Brace & Jovanovich, Inc.

_____, 1972. Soma and the Fly-agaric—Mr. Wasson's rejoiner to Professor Brough. *Bot. Mus.* Harvard Univ., Cambridge, Mass.

Weil, A.T., 1972. *The Natural Mind: A New Way of Looking at Drugs and the Higher Consciousness.* Houghton Mifflin Co., Boston, Mass.

Wolbach, A.B. Jr. Isbell, H., & Miner, E.J., 1962. Comparison of psilocin with psilocybin, mescaline and LSD-25. *Psychopharmacol.* 3:219–223.

Wooley, D.W., & Campbell, N.K., 1962. Serotonin-like and antiserotonin properties of psilocybin and psilocin. *Science* 136:777–778.

Zsigmond, E.K., Folders, V.M., & Folders, F.F., 1963. The *in vitro* inhibitory effect of psilocybin and related compounds on human cholinesterases. *Psychopharmacol.* 4:232–234.

Galerina autumnalis   POISONOUS

Amanita phalloides   POISONOUS

Amanita muscaria ①

Amanita pantherina ②

Gymnopilus spectabilis ⑤

Panaeolina foenisecii ⑥

Panaeolus acuminatus ⑦

Panaeolus castaneifolius ⑨

Panaeolus campanulatus ⑧

Panaeolus fimicola ⑩

Panaeolus retirugis ⑬

Panaeolus phalaenarum ⑫

Panaeolus semiovatus (14)

Panaeolus subbalteatus (16)

◄*Panaeolus subbalteatus* (16)

Psilocybe baeocystis (17)

Psilocybe baeocystis   Removing Pellicle

Psilocybe baeocystis ⑰

Psilocybe coprophila ⑱

Psilocybe cubensis   Cultivated (19)

Psilocybe cyanescens (20)

Psilocybe cyanescens (20)

Psilocybe pelliculosa ㉑

Psilocybe semilanceata ㉒

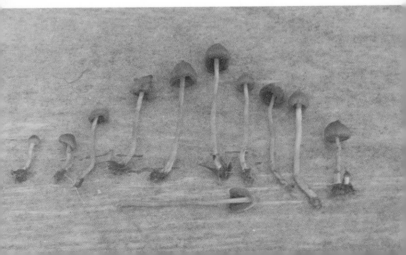

Psilocybe semilanceata (22)

Psilocybe strictipes (23)

Psilocybe stuntzii (24)

Psilocybe stuntzii (24)